WHO KILLED
DONNA GENTILE ?

THE REAL STORY

Larry S. Avrech

Adamos Novus Books

CONTENTS

———————

Disclaimer

Adamo Novus Books is an imprint of Focus7 Publishing under the parent company Focus7 Consulting and is a service provider(s), not a publishing house.

As a service provider, we are not responsible for the information, opinions, and/or claims in this book.

The author is solely responsible for the accuracy of any statement(s), opinions, claims, indications, names mentioned, or information presented in this work.

We do not back or agree/disagree with any of the information, opinions, and/or claims made in the documents or writing. The service provider(s) is not liable for any damages or negative consequences to any person in the book or to any person reading or acting upon the information in this book.

References are provided for informational purposes only and do not constitute endorsement of any websites, authors, or other sources. Readers should be aware that the websites listed in this book may change.

DEDICATION

I would like to thank my parents,
Bernard and Mildred Avrech *for raising me to
understand the difference between right and wrong,
never to quit no matter how the odds were stacked
against me and no goal was out of reach.*

———

I would also like to thank **Richard J. Lewis** *for the tremendous
insight and knowledge he bestowed upon me. Without his assistance, I
might well have been accused of a crime I didn't commit.*

*He allowed the playing field to be leveled for me and gave me an equal
opportunity neither the people of San Diego, my Police Department or
the media would provide. Thank you for believing in me and allowing
me to help you with a most complex case.*

"Failure is success in progress."
Albert Einstein

FOREWORD

In general, the death of a prostitute typically garners little media attention. Who cares? She's one of life's expendable, perhaps tragic, invisible people. She's simply another life lost on the street. However, when a prostitute contacts major media outlets to tell her story, and is subsequently brutally beaten to death and dumped on the side of a road like so much trash, the media narrative and coverage change. Suddenly, this prostitute's murder is front page news and implicates in various ways, San Diego law enforcement.

This is the story of the gruesome murder of Donna Marie Gentile. Some would view her as a $20-a-trick street whore murdered by a "John." Some would see her involvement, occasionally intimate, with law enforcement and suggest she was their victim. Involvement, even intimate, doesn't prove guilt, but the flurry of media gossip suggested every possibility and innuendo to sell the media side. Donna was a sister, a daughter, an aunt. She was a loved member of a family. She was a real person. No matter who killed Donna Gentile or how she was thought of in life, she didn't deserve the horrible death inflicted upon her. Who killed her and what are the insidious details behind the media stories? All is told here.

You may wonder how I'm involved in writing this Foreword. Well, Larry asked me and I accepted. Simple as that. I was Larry Avrech's Sergeant on the San Diego Police Department at the time some of these events took place. I thought highly of Larry then as I do now. When I took time off from work, I placed him in charge of the squad for days and sometimes weeks at a time. He was and is smart, knowledgeable, honest, and diligent. He always did an admirable job as an officer and acting Sergeant. After Donna Gentile was killed, many, including police, were suspected of some involvement, no matter how tangential. Her badly beaten body was dumped in San Diego County. Thus, jurisdiction of the homicide fell to the San Diego Sheriff's Office. As the reader will see, the dual jurisdiction between City and County assisted those seeking to misrepresent facts and derail the investigation. I was ordered by my command at the San Diego Police Department to be interrogated by Sheriff's Homicide Detective Tom Streed. Streed has a degree in behavioral science with a reputation of having special insight and abilities in conducting interrogations. Personally, I found Streed to be elementary and not capable of managing an in-depth interview.

This fascinating, fast-paced account, keeps the reader hooked, awaiting the next page. The controversies surrounding this San Diego County case intensified from week to week as local law enforcement personnel were implicated as suspects and witnesses. Larry Avrech's acumen as a detective, attention to detail, and integrity for the truth will thrill and entice you to keep reading to the end. He wades through the official deliberate deceptions to tell the well-documented truthful behind-the-scenes action in which he was personally involved from the beginning. Few people knew he was working closely with a Deputy District Attorney who would later lead the San Diego Metropolitan Homicide Task Force.

During the course of his investigation, Larry was maligned on nearly all angles. He lost his home, became nomadic, living in his car, and moving from place to place with temporary employment.

Homicide detectives are portrayed as heroes onscreen. However, no on-screen character and few writers have spent enough time on the streets to step behind the screen and show us how detectives operate. Larry Avrech was a street cop, a damn good street cop. He wasn't a formal police homicide detective, yet his stellar accomplishments resulted in revelations about the Donna Gentile homicide even the best and brightest in the San Diego Sheriff's Office were unable to expose.

This story documents how our system of justice can be easily exploited and damaged for the benefit of the few and to the detriment of many. If Larry Avrech played a small part in righting some of these wrongs, he will have been successful in his role as an investigator and author. Read on. I guarantee you will wish for more. This is a true story. The people are real. The facts are documented.

Connie D. Zimmerman

Sergeant, San Diego Police Department, Retired

ACKNOWLEDGMENTS

The writing of this book was a long and tedious journey, but more enriching and fulfilling than I could've imagined.

None of this would've been possible without my friends in uniform, who refused to be intimidated. You all know who you are and will remain nameless for obvious reasons. I thank you all.

Above all, I wish to thank God. Without God, I wouldn't be here to write this book.

———

I wish to thank the following people for helping me see through, to the writing of this book, to realize my dream and allow it to become a reality. To the following people, I salute you.

I wish to thank my parents Bernard (+) and Mildred Avrech, (+) the Angels on my shoulders who guided me through the writing of this book.

To Richard (Dick) J. Lewis, (+) retired Deputy District Attorney of

San Diego County, Life Saver, Teacher, Father figure and Best friend, who gave me the courage, insight and determination to fight a system and prevail.

I wish to thank Connie D. Zimmerman, retired Sergeant, San Diego Police Department, Attorney and close friend, who encouraged me to write this book, wrote the Foreword for this book and had my back throughout this never-ending nightmare.

To Nancy Lee Avrech, my loving wife and companion, for her spiritual and technical support and for being my sounding board.

I would like to thank Denise Michaels, book coach and founder of International Writing Guild for smoothing out the rough edges and facilitating its construction.

I would also like to thank Lisa Frederickson of Focus 7 Consulting, for publishing my book, cover design, formatting and landing page construction.

To Karissa Skirmont of Profoundly Purple, for her expert skills in the construction of my Website and her technical advice.

I wish to thank Samuel Carpenter, Director/Producer of Adventum Productions for his Photography and Video Production.

To John Stryker-Meyer, retired San Diego Union Newspaper Reporter, Author, friend who followed my case and believed in me and was a positive driving force for me in a negative newspaper world.

To Jon Standefer (+) retired San Diego Union Newspaper Reporter, friend who initiated the ball rolling and helped introduce me to others who would connect me with the District Attorney's Office.

I wish to thank Donald Hardy (+) retired Homicide Sergeant, San Bernardino Sheriff's Department/Polygrapher, friend, who introduced me to Dick Lewis in the District Attorney's Office.

I would also like to thank Rich Bonin, producer at 60 *Minutes*, who met with me and gave me the name of a local reporter in San Diego I could trust to hear me out and run my story.

To the Honorable Charles G. Rogers, San Diego Superior Court Judge/Former Deputy District Attorney, Author, who came out of retirement to initially head the San Diego Metropolitan Homicide Task Force, for believing in me and providing spiritual support.

To John Troy Morrison, retired Lieutenant, San Diego Police Department, Speaker, Author, friend for his emotional and technical support and believing in me.

To Jack Tague, (+) retired Sergeant, San Diego Police Department/Homicide Investigator/District Attorney Investigator, my First Field Training Officer Sergeant and friend who believed in me and for his continued support and efforts to hire me on another Police Department.

I wish to thank Richard Keith Boas (+) retired Lieutenant San Diego Police Department, friend, for his continued support and technical advice.

(+) denotes deceased

Without these individuals help and determination, this book would not be possible.

I thank you all,

Larry S. Avrech

INTRODUCTION

Who killed Donna Gentile? A known San Diego prostitute who gravitated to San Diego from Levittown, Pennsylvania after dropping out of high school and being molested by her stepfather at home. After arriving in San Diego, she was unable to find work and resorted to prostitution. She quickly learned the talk of the streets and became savvy, streetwise and able to easily manipulate people.

After several arrests she learned to leverage her exposure time by befriending San Diego Police Officers in an attempt to exercise a form of control over. In times of need, Gentile would turn officers in to police authorities when she needed favors on her pending cases.

Gentile played both sides of the street by turning in officers and plying her trade at the same time. The San Diego police department was aware of this; yet allowed it to continue.

She became the number one problem on El Cajon Boulevard, when prostitution was completely out of control. So, the City was asked to put a special prostitution enforcement detail requiring additional officers assigned to the area along with money and to combat this problem over time. Most of the prostitutes left the area and went to other areas of the city, some left town completely. But when the smoke cleared there was Donna Gentile who was referred to as a "die hard" prostitute who stayed on and continued to defy the law.

Lieutenant Carl Black, an Eastern Division Lieutenant was placed in charge of this detail. In less than three months, Black became involved with Gentile and she would call for him when officers stopped her on the Boulevard.

On a traffic stop, I found this out from Gentile herself, when she told me she was being harassed by cops. But the harassment would come to an end soon, because she had a Lieutenant in her hip pocket.

During this time Gentile attempted to place me in highly compromising situations, but I kept my distance, resisting her advances. Once I felt possible corruption existed between Black and Gentile, I felt I needed to investigate whether this was true or not. I took the advice of one of my Sergeants who I believed I could trust and was told I need to verify the truth or falsehood of the matter. After all, if my suspicions were untrue it could damage a career. I continued communication with Gentile by phone and in the field.

Additional contact revealed she indeed was involved with my Lieutenant but to what extent was still unknown. Gentile told me she was going on a four-day trip to the Colorado River with Black and some friends. Later it was determined Gentile indeed went to the river with Black and was fixed up with Black's Sergeant friend, Ken Hargrove. They were old buddies who worked together when Black made Sergeant years ago. Both were in trouble with women before, but the department chose to handle it quietly. Once Gentile realized she was giving information about Black's involvement with her and she wasn't getting anything from me and she couldn't manipulate me, she resorted to lying and making false accusations about my conduct which ultimately led to my dismissal from the force.

Throughout the investigation, the department decided to believe Gentile, who had credibility issues. I didn't, but they chose to believe her over me, "Because it fit the specific needs of the department at that particular time."

Carl Black was investigated as well, but he seemed to live a charmed life, considering his past discipline on the department. He was ultimately fired for other acts discovered by investigators which he neglected to tell them. Black appealed his termination with the Chief of Police and was reinstated, but he was reduced in rank for one year. In contrast, I was terminated after my Chief's appeal with a Deputy Chief not of my choosing.

After testifying at my Civil Service hearing, Gentile was found murdered, her body dumped in the Mount Laguna area of East San Diego County.

But who killed Donna Gentile? It looked as if she was retaliated against for her testimony against me. Was it Carl Black? Was it someone on the Police Department? A John?

This isn't just the story of Donna Gentile. It's primarily the story of how a good cop's life was turned upside down when suddenly everything went horribly wrong after his brief contact with her, and, at the eleventh hour how everything suddenly went right.

Throughout this exciting thriller, I'll take you from the murder scene back to the beginning of this case, through the continued harassment I experienced from Internal Affairs even after my termination. You'll feel the agonizing pain at the loss of my career, home, children, marriage, car and my loving pets. How did I survive? How did I clear myself?

I was tried by the newspapers and electronic media, as well as by the people of San Diego. I also was alienated from my friends on the department for fear the department might retaliate against them; living from place to place sometimes out of my car, barely surviving.

I possessed the strength and conviction to someday, somehow solve the case of who killed Donna Gentile and remove the dark cloud which followed me like a shadow for years.

This case was a scab over a wound never given a chance to heal. Every so often, the media would pick at the scab and make it bleed all over again. It seemed important enough to bring up the case a year after I was terminated and again a year after Donna Gentile's death. Then on the anniversaries of her death up to 30 years later, when finally a book was published by a family member of Gentile, further propagating the misinformation and opinions of others who weren't there and didn't live it as I did.

Finally, it happened. In the spring of 1986, I received a call from a high-ranking Deputy District Attorney who said, "Larry I've been following your case and you don't have a sour grapes case. You were set up by your department and I can prove it."

For the next seven years I secretly met with Richard J. Lewis from the District Attorney's Office. Nothing about the Gentile murder or the other Task Force cases was kept from me. Nobody knew about me, not the media, the District Attorney (until 1999) or anyone else from law enforcement. I was the most closely-guarded secret in San Diego.

I provided a suspect, who was under the radar at the time, as far as a suspect was concerned in the Gentile murder case as well as in 13 other murders.

In this book I promise to take you from the murder scene, through the investigation to the eventual outcome. I'll share the true story. There is no guesswork or supposition in this book.

As you read, your mind will be quenched with each page you turn. As you continue reading, you'll see what my eyes saw and what my ears heard as if you were there yourself. This book was written in the hope of connecting with other people who know of an officer or who was an officer drawn into a similar controversy.

After almost thirty-five years isn't it time for the truth to be known?

Buckle up and get ready to take a fast-paced trip through the workings of one of the most successful serial killing Task Forces in the Country.

PART ONE

CHAPTER ONE

A BODY IS FOUND

SAN DIEGO, East County is where I reside, just 62.1 miles from the epicenter of a thriving metropolis, where over two million people live.

It's June 22, 1985, a typically perfect day in Mt. Laguna. The high temperature was 82 degrees and the next day the mercury shot up to 91 degrees.

The area is surrounded by igneous rock, formed and crystalized thousands of years ago from volcanos. The boulders jut out from the Manzanita, tangled, thorny chaparral and sagebrush as the elevation stretches up to almost 6,000 feet above sea level. Visitors hear an occasional car drive by this scenic route and the faint sounds of traffic in the distance on Interstate 8.

Then in a turnout, off this county road, campers and truckers pull off the road to spend the night. Marring the natural beauty, there's dirt, broken glass bottles, tin cans and bits of paper strewn everywhere. Tonight, along with the trash, was the lifeless body of a young woman, dumped like another piece of discarded trash. She was nude with her clothes piled on her abdomen; her pale cold skin exposed to the night. Blotchy bruises already gray with death covered her neck and face. Her deep brown hair swept across her forehead with the soft, summer breezes.

The expression on her youthful face was one of resignation in the dim moonlit sky. There was no identification on or near the body, she was a nameless young woman who played with fire and lost. The question was, who murdered her?

A passerby out for a run, exercising his dog, discovered the body. He notified the authorities at about eight o'clock in the evening. Once the San Diego Sheriff's department was on the scene the standard protocol was completed. This involved assessing the scene, limiting the number of people allowed inside the perimeter, while making sketches and photographing the surrounding area. Photographs of the body were taken, while looking for any trace or evidence of impressions such as footprints or tire tracks. Evidence was collected, measurements were taken and the body was rolled over to check for additional wounds or abnormalities. Her clothing was preserved along with her personal effects. Finally, the hands and feet were bagged before transporting the body to the morgue.

Once at the Medical Examiner's office, fingernail clipping samples were taken, along with more photographs. Bodily fluids are collected, tissue samples taken, and note is made of any scars or tattoos. Fingerprints are taken in an attempt to identify the deceased. If an autopsy isn't performed immediately, the body is put on ice.

The daily newspaper, the San Diego Union, printed a small blurb in the June 25, 1985 morning edition. Police found the nude body of an unidentified white female in her twenties in the Pine Valley area. An autopsy would be performed.*

On July 3, 1985, upon returning home from a hearing, I noticed a flashing light on my answering machine, a device everyone attached to our home phones long before we all became addicted to smartphones. There was a message from a Channel 8 reporter and friend, Dave Cohen. He was one of the few reporters who listened to my story. He even drove out to my comic book store to talk with me. He also was kind enough to give me fifty dollars, so I could buy groceries to feed my kids. My children are now grown, but my daughter was seven and my son was six back in 1985.

Dave's haunting message stated, "Larry, it's Dave Cohen from Channel 8. I hope you're not planning on suing Donna Gentile. They just found her body a few days ago in Pine Valley."

A cold chill ran through my body. I thought the brief article I saw eight days ago could be Gentile, but I wasn't sure and couldn't check.

My immediate thought was, oh my God they killed her to frame me. I just became an instant murder suspect. Law enforcement today likes to sugar coat the word "suspect" and today suspects are often called a "person of interest." But let's not fool ourselves, though I was miles away from Gentile and last saw her at my Civil Service hearing in May, I was now a bona fide murder suspect.

The local agencies, the Sheriff's Department and the San Diego Police Department were not commenting, but their silence was every bit as damning. My heart felt like it was beating out of my chest. I slumped in a kitchen chair, leaning forward with my hands over both temples. Visibly shaken, I sat for a few minutes trying to compose myself. After a few minutes I got up and tried calling my attorney. But I was so nervous, I couldn't hit the right numbers on my phone dial pad as my hands shook. Finally, I reached him and told him what I just heard.

"He said, Oh my goodness! I can't believe it." He instructed me to stay in touch with him and not speak to anyone about Gentile's death.

Local news shows led every program with the grisly news, my picture plastered all over television and the papers. People were hastily putting two plus two together and coming up with the wrong conclusion. They were starting to suspect I killed her. They wrongly assumed Officer Avrech associated with her, she turned him in, testified against him and now she's dead. In their minds an open and shut case. It was an easy conclusion to make because on the surface it made sense. But it wasn't true and suddenly I was in a fight for my life.

The July 4, 1985, morning edition of the San Diego Union made a positive identification through local fingerprints on file; the body was indeed that of Donna Marie Gentile.*

Perhaps somehow, she knew this would eventually be her fate. Any dreams she might've hoped for in her short, thorny life, despite her profession as a prostitute, were now snuffed out. No second chances to turn things around and get it right.

On July 6, 1985, a piece in the San Diego Union written by reporter friend Dick Weber indicated Gentile made a tape-recorded statement last March about her fear of being killed. She made the tape the day before going into custody for 55 days on a prostitution conviction. It was given to her attorney, Douglas Holbrook, who gave it to reporter Bob Donley from KGTV News. Donley played it for homicide detectives.

On the tape Gentile stated, "I have no intention of disappearing or going out of town without letting my lawyer know first." She said, "Because of the publicity I've received in the police scandal, this is why I am making this tape. I feel that even a person in uniform with a badge can still be a serious criminal. This is the only life insurance I have."

I couldn't grasp what was happening. As a young San Diego Police Officer, I was looking forward to a great career and doing what I thought was right for the department and my community. I was hired to uphold the law and protect the citizens of San Diego. I truly believed in that standard of service. When I saw activity conflicting with my moral fiber, I felt a duty to investigate and turn my findings over to the proper departmental investigative branch.

The media later informed the public she was found nude, lying on her back with her clothes piled on top of her. Gentile's mouth was filled with rocks and gravel. She was beaten about the head and her neck and back were broken in three places when her body was found. The news media had a field day claiming her mouth was filled with rocks and gravel because she was snitch and this was the killer's punishment for talking.

I always felt and it can be shown in the following cases: In Russia between 1978-1990 a serial killer named Andrei Chikatilo, who killed as many as 56 persons was tried and executed for 52 murders. He was known as the Butcher of Rostov, the Red Ripper and the Rostov Ripper. His method of killing varied, but often his victim's mouths were stuffed with dirt and mud. This was done to stifle their screaming. None of his victims were informants.*

Closer to home, in San Diego, in 1978 and 1984 respectively two murders took place at Torrey Pines State Beach. Barbara Nantais, age 15 was strangled, beaten and sand was put in her mouth. Six years later Claire Hough, age 14 was brutally murdered. Sand was also found in her mouth. Neither of these victims were informants. This proves my theory. The use of rocks, gravel, sand, mud and dirt was merely a method used to stifle their screams. Donna Gentile was also found with rocks and gravel in her mouth to stifle her screams.

Donna Gentile was a police informant, something the department didn't want to admit. She continued committing crimes while she worked as an active prostitute in direct violation of informant procedures. The San Diego Police Department knew it. Plus, she tried to use Carl Black as a "Sugar Daddy."

Gentile realized if Black were turned in, she would lose her source of money he provided her. So, she went to Internal Affairs with trumped up allegations about me, ultimately costing me my job and career in Law Enforcement.

Despite her manipulation and deceit, no one should die the way she did. If I was to clear myself, I had to get to the bottom of the case. But how?

In order to understand my connection to Donna Marie Gentile, we must turn the clock back and start where the story begins.

———

*Denotes Documents or Photos which are available at www.whokilleddonnagentile.com/extras

** Denotes Book or Periodical found in Book Bibliography and/or www.whokilleddonnagentile.com/extras

CHAPTER TWO

THE EARLY DAYS

In 1976, I decided to become a sworn San Diego Police Officer. I discovered it was a long, drawn-out process. First, to qualify for the position, you must be at least 20.5-years old, with a clean criminal record, be in good physical health, good vision and no marijuana or cocaine use in the last two years. The last requirement may be shocking to some people. However, it became difficult to fill police academy classes with candidates who never experimented with those drugs. In addition to those requirements, I had to pass a physical exam by a City of San Diego doctor, pass a polygraph examination and a physical agility test.

During the late seventies and early eighties, it became necessary to expand the current sworn personnel of the San Diego Police Department. A study showed there were about 1.3 police officers per one thousand residents in San Diego, when there should be two police officers per thousand. Despite hiring practices and bigger budget allotments, the city was still grappling with the problem. The police academy was grinding out 100 candidates per academy class, every six weeks. Unfortunately, it was never quite enough to make up for the current officers who were fired, transferred to other assignments, promoted, injured and retired.

For most candidates, the academy was a grueling four-and-a-half-month program. I was hired in November of 1979 after being a reserve officer for three years. During that stretch, I worked under-cover narcotics and was assigned to the robbery division in addition to riding as a second officer in a patrol unit. When I was hired, it was a revolving door for me as I turned in my reserve gear one day only to pick up my sworn officer gear the next day. I was finally hired full-time with a paycheck.

Some candidates who were physically fit but couldn't handle the academics and the reverse was also true. From the 100 candidates we started with in our class, only 53 of us graduated. Others were weeded out for such things as low scholastic averages, failing a test and failing the remediation test, cheating and carrying a concealed weapon.

The curriculum in the academy was intense, students were tested in as many as 15 different subjects at a time and we were only allowed to fail one test for the entire program. If the academy staff felt you were worth remediation, you could get a break and be retested. Otherwise, you fell by the wayside and were booted out of the academy.

The San Diego Police Academy was run like a para-military opera-tion. It was yes sir, no sir, permission to enter the academy staff office sir and so on. Occasionally, people forgot their place, but they were quickly reminded by the staff and got back in line.

There were two physical tests most found difficult. One was a vertical stair climb with a person strapped to a gurney. During my academy, the department still operated police ambulances. The stair climb was an exercise where one man was strapped to a gurney and carried up three flights of 21 steps each with two landings, for a total of 63 steps. Another challenge was the wall climb. We were required to run up three flights of 21 steps each, jump over a three-foot hurdle, get over a four-foot wall and then, scale a six-foot wall. Once over the wall, recruits had to pick up a weighted dummy of about 150 pounds and drag it across a designated finish line. Finally, we simulated cuffing a suspect by holding a dummy with spring-loaded PVC arms and holding them together for about 15 seconds.

I enjoyed my academy days. The daily physical training involved running anywhere from one to six miles. Prior to entering the academy, I practiced running up and down the escalators at Jack Murphy Stadium. I knew a few security officers there and they allowed me inside to practice during non-business hours

I entered the academy in the first week of November 1979. No sooner was I there when physical or PT training started. One of our first runs was up a parking lot hill. The academy staffer leading the run, instructed us to roll our feet when running uphill. He mentioned, "You might be a little sore the next day." On November 13, 1979, while running the 440-yard dash in PT class, I felt a sharp pain sear through both legs. As I was finishing the race, I was unable to stand firmly.

I was sent to a city doctor who diagnosed me as having shin splints. He told me I must suspend any running for two weeks.* I hoped this wouldn't interfere with my academy status. I thought all the training I did prior to being hired would've been enough to get me in tip-top shape. I was told to ice my shins down several times a day until the pain and swelling subsided. I returned to full duty on December 22' 1979 but was behind the rest of the class in physical training. I still needed to complete all the PT tests, including running an eight-minute mile. Fortunately I finished all the tests with flying colors

Scholastically, I did fine, despite the fact I was unable to devote as much time to studying as I wanted. My 16-month old son was having seizures due to a fever as a result of chronic ear infections and was rushed to the hospital. He needed tubes put in his ears. Consequently, I lost a lot of sleep and study time being a young father. Going over my class notes combined with my police reserve experience, I ended up graduating 17th in my class of 100 with a 91.6 percent score.

I was filled with pride at the thought of becoming a full -fledged San Diego Police Officer. My graduation was scheduled for March 3, 1980 at the Scottish Rite Temple in Mission Valley. My parents, relatives and friends were incredibly proud of me as well.

I would've liked it even more if my parents were able to attend. However, my mother was recently diagnosed with Multiple Sclerosis and was unable to travel. My in-laws, Al and Helen Alsop* attended along with my wife, Susan. My best friend and reserve partner Jeff Bambara* also attended. Jeff and I were reserve officers together before being hired as sworn officers. He graduated three months ahead of me. After receiving my graduation certificate, I posed for a picture with *Chief Bill Kolender.

PROBATIONARY STATUS

As a police officer in San Diego, once you finish the academy, you're placed with a field training officer, or "FTO" for four one-month periods, working different divisions each month at different shift times.

My first phase was out of the Northern Division working the graveyard shift in Pacific Beach and La Jolla. My FTO was Charles "Chuck" Montierth. At this point in time, I made my first DUI arrest. I pulled over a woman who was driving erratically. Upon stopping her she rolled up her windows and wouldn't get out of her car. She finally rolled down the window on the passenger side enough for us to open the door and remove her from the car. She wouldn't submit to a coordination test and became combative. As I tried to restrain her, she bit my right forearm. She was cuffed and taken to jail by another unit while I drove to Mission Bay Hospital for a Tetanus shot. My Supervisor was Jack Tague. He was a phenomenal homicide detective for years before returning to patrol. He went with me to the hospital and after rolling up my sleeve for the shot, the nurse said, "Nope drop 'em."

After the shot Tague said, "We need to fill out some paperwork so let's go to Shelton's for coffee." I successfully passed my first phase of training.

Another FTO on the squad was Mike Burstein. He used to make snide comments about me being "the new kid on the block." When I finished my last shift at Northern Division, I was in the locker room when he came up to me and said, "Hey kid, I didn't want to give you a swelled head or anything, but you sure know what you're doing out there."

Mike and I remained friends after I left the department. In April of 1999, I unfortunately had to attend his son's funeral. His son Steve, a motor officer, was killed while off duty in a traffic accident on his way to meet his father in the desert.

My second phase was in the Ocean Beach/Point Loma area on the graveyard. My FTO was Don Harris. Don lived two blocks over from me and we car-pooled to work. One of the cases we handled was a roof top burglary of a jewelry store in Ocean Beach. The suspects chopped a hole in the roof and used a pair of 2x4's nailed together in crisscross fashion. A garden hose was used to lower the suspects inside. When the owner of the shop arrived in the morning, he pointed to a flashlight left at the scene. He asked, "Can you get any prints off that?" It was a silver metal fluted "Eveready Captains flashlight."

Harris said to forget it, we couldn't raise any prints off the fluted metal.

I opened the flashlight and printed the batteries. As it turned out, the store owner's prints were all over the batteries. He later admitted to detectives he hired others to burglarize his store, so he could collect insurance money on a false claim. My FTO Sergeant at the time was Dave Stanley. Both Stanley and Harris thought this should be reflected in my evaluation. The evaluation form scores ranged from 1-5. Nobody ever got a 5 but they decided this was an exception and I was given a 5.

Later, detectives told me they never would've thought to print the batteries inside the flashlight to solve the case.

My third phase was working the DUI squad, a special drunk driving squad, whose main function was to stop and evaluate people for driving under the influence. My FTO. was Mike Miller who I replaced at the University of San Diego's Campus police, when he was hired by the city. I handled a fatal accident where for the first time I experienced what brain matter looked like. I also handled a police equipment accident in addition to arresting drunk drivers and getting them off the road.

The San Diego department placed a great deal of emphasis on traffic enforcement. They discovered a direct relationship between the number of accidents, the number of drunk driving arrests and the number of traffic citations written. As a result, San Diego enjoyed one of the lowest auto insurance rates in the state.

My fourth phase was in Eastern Division. My FTO was Gary Slocum. There were two Slocum's on the Department, Rick and Gary. Gary was nicknamed "Smokin' Slocum." In a regular eight hour shift he'd switch from cigarettes to his "Optimo Palma" cigars to a pipe. He certainly lived up to his nickname. It was easy to distinguish between the two Slocums. Rumor had it, he wound up with all the problem recruits. As it happened, he was the only officer available on the squad. I learned a lot from Gary, and he gave me additional handouts and reading assignments. I was a non-smoker, so I learned from him in between coughing jags. My FTO Sergeant was Fred

Moeller. Halfway through training, Moeller let me take the unit out by myself. He and Slocum followed me to my calls. I needed minimal supervision.

At the time, I lived in the Eastern Division area and worked it as a Reserve Officer. So, I knew the area like the back of my hand. I successfully completed my phase training and received notice I would be assigned to Northeastern Division.

Once released from the phase training program, officers are on a probationary status and evaluated monthly by their Sergeant. You skate on thin ice, ducking and dodging any citizen complaints, poor test grades, bad police procedures and personality conflicts with supervisors.

The Northeastern Division is a more affluent area of the city with fewer crime problems. I would've rather worked the Eastern area where every type of crime occurs. There were crimes in progress, narcotics, robberies, thefts, bookmaking, prostitution, burglaries, child neglect and abuse, domestic violence and more. I preferred to be where the action was. I went down to personnel to ask Sergeant Hoffman if there were any criteria used when assigning officers to a particular area. I asked Hoffman if I could switch with someone from my academy class. He pointed to a name which turned out to be Greg McClendon. He said, "How about him?"

I said, "He was the class clown and didn't know his left foot from his right when marching. He was constantly out of step.

Hoffman said, "No problem." He took a bottle of White Out and whited out the "N" for Northeastern next to my name and wrote in an" N" next to McClendon's name. He said, "You've just been reassigned to Eastern Division. I shook his hand, thanked him and left his office. Greg McClendon's name will figure prominently later in the book.

As a result of writing a large numbers of citations, the department encouraged officers to maintain what they considered well-rounded activity. This, meaning a variety of arrests, report writing, citizen contacts, field interrogations or "FI" along with parking citations and traffic citations as previously mentioned.

An FI is contact with a subject you suspect is likely to or has just committed a crime. The primary idea behind FIs is to accurately document an individual at a specific place, time and date and the reason and crime potential this person poses to the community. For example, a juvenile out past curfew can pose a lot of problems. This person can be considered a suspect of a crime for being in the wrong place at the wrong time. He could also be a crime victim by not being indoors at 10:00 pm. In this instance, we take this person home and notify a parent to find out why he/she was out past curfew. There may be a domestic problem at home where police can intervene and provide a referral for family counseling. Nevertheless, we put the FI in the Automated Regional Justice Information System (ARJIS) computer for six months to let other officers be aware of previous contacts with law enforcement.

A good cop uses the computer at the end of his shift to see if the person he contacted has a history of other contacts or arrests with law enforcement. Another example is contacting a person who loiters around school yards; the crime potential could encompass anything from kidnapping, child stealing, child molestation or narcotics.

Where I worked on El Cajon Boulevard in east San Diego, daily problems of school truancy, gang activity, daytime burglaries, bank robberies, auto thefts, narcotics, criminal assaults and prostitution were found. Some people say prostitution is a victimless crime. However, the majority of prostitutes in San Diego work for a pimp: an individual who derives support or maintenance in whole or in part from the earnings or proceeds of a prostitute.

In 1980 prostitution was running rampant in San Diego. As a result, prostitutes stole from their "Johns" or "tricks."

Besides having well-rounded activity, other things can satisfy your FTO Sergeant responsible for your evaluation and make your probation. You can take an interest in the area where you work by contacting merchants and citizens and finding out what you can do as an officer to solve the complaints of the community. For example, in a high crime area, the department was successful implementing a community alert neighborhood watch group in neighborhoods across the city. An officer can provide public speaking opportunities and set up watch groups, assisting citizens with home security ideas to make their home or business safer from intrusion.

Another tool the department used was the citizen "Ride-A-Long" program. A citizen who lives or works in a specific area can ride with a beat officer. Citizens are given an education after one of these rides. They learn how the department's priority system works and why a citizen might wait several hours for a police officer to show up and take a report. There are five priorities from one being a life-threatening call or crime in progress; to five, a citizen contact regarding a neighborhood problem or a blocked driveway. So, an officer who shows well-rounded activity, is a "team player," who stays out of trouble and gets along with supervision should successfully complete probation.

As a police reserve officer from 1976-1979, I achieved a head start in the academy as I watched other probationary officers make mistakes and learn the correct way to handle certain situations as I did years prior. It certainly helped me in the academy as I was described by the academy staff as a role model for others.*

I was assigned to Eastern Division. At the time there were seven divisions in the city. Eastern Division encompasses approximately 67.2 square miles* Interstate 8 is one of the boundaries, an east-west interstate freeway traveling from Ocean Beach, California east to the junction with Interstate 10 at Casa Grande, Arizona. The eastern units working north of I-8 encounter different activity than the units working south of the freeway. On the north side is Navy housing, juvenile problems, domestic violence, residential and commercial burglaries some robberies, auto thefts, sex crimes and child abuse.

In Eastern Division, I worked and grew familiar with all the beats. Working north of the freeway you could receive a total of two or three radio calls a night in an eight-hour shift and get off work on time every evening. Working south of the freeway was a different world all together. Officers go from call to call and writing a rough journal. Most days after your shift, your journal would be completed. I was constantly involved in arrests, narcotic impounds, or crime reports carrying me past my shift. I handled a double rape which occurred 20 minutes before the end of my shift. I put in 11 hours of overtime on those reports before all the paperwork was completed. My motto was, "I work eight hours or whatever it takes to get the job done." I was a perfectionist and a digger, leaving no stone unturned.

When I graduated from the academy, I set a goal to put in 20-25 years and retire as a Lieutenant in charge of an investigative bureau. As you'll see this was cut short.

My academy was the last class to require a two-year probationary period. Mine was reduced two months when I was notified in January of 1982 my probation would end at the end of the month. After making probation, I continued in the department until January 22, 1985.

WHEN I FIRST HAD A TARGET ON MY BACK

Once you're assigned in phase training, officers are issued a "Critical Task Booklet." It contains different field situations to be completed and signed off by the FTO. These tasks range from traffic stops to report writing, radio use, traffic citations, field interrogations and impounding narcotics or found property. To receive the first six-month step raise, the booklet must be completed and returned to the field training office after finishing your fourth phase.

Despite carrying this out to the letter, in September of 1980, we didn't receive our six-month step raise until the following month. Thinking the situation would correct itself in the next six months, once again, we were forced to wait an additional month to April of 1981 for our raise. Now, concerned this would continue every six months, I started hearing from my academy classmates telling me the city wasn't paying them the correct rate either.

While in the academy, the staff provided us with a procedure for challenging answers to exam questions. When someone thought they should be given credit for an answer they felt was more correct than the answer key, the staff told us to pick one person in the class to write the challenge stating his reasons why another answer was better. Once submitted to the academy office, the staff would decide to either throw out the question or give credit to all. Since I was the only person in the class with Reserve Officer experience they asked me, "Larry, you know how to write these reports. Will you write a challenge for us?"

I told them I would even though my answer was correct. I did this about six times which gave the class extra test points. I never lost a challenge. Sometimes it meant the difference between someone getting an A instead of a B, a C or a failing grade. I don't recall all the questions I challenged but one was so ridiculous it needed to be changed. It was a multiple-choice question where the choice for "C" was none of the above and "D" was all the above.

My final evaluation from the academy* stated, "Avrech has an eye for detail and frequently points out inconsistences on poorly written materials such as tests and handouts."

This time I was asked to write a grievance on behalf of my academy class and I graciously accepted.

At the time, I was working for Sergeant Rulette Armstead, an attractive black woman. She listened to my account and beside myself this issue affected 24 other officers from my academy class. Armstead wrote an eight-page memorandum* on March 31, 1981 and sent it up the chain to the acting Lieutenant Rod Quigley. Quigley sent it to the FTO administration. It was sent to Lieutenant Tom Hall. Hall was my academy Sergeant when I went through the Reserve Academy in 1976 and later the Lieutenant who interviewed me for my sworn position with the city and hired me in 1979. I received an interoffice memo from Hall on April 22, 1981, * saying he would do his best to expedite the matter. He later became my Captain at Eastern Division who recommended my termination in 1985.

I obtained a Police Officer Association attorney, Chris Ashcraft. On May 8,1981, Hall denied the request, but it was agreed it needed to be sent to the City Management Team. On May 29, 1981, while waiting for a decision from the City Management Team, I received a memo from Commander Don Davis who also denied the grievance, on the grounds it wasn't filed in a timely manner. On June 15, Ashcraft and I met with Chief Ken O'Brien to determine the validity of the grievance.* After a long session with the Chief he felt there was some substance to the grievance. O'Brien would figure later as the Chief who heard my appeal for reinstatement prior to my final termination. He wasn't my first choice. I requested Chief Kolender and was told he was out of town the next week. As I walked out to the parking lot I noticed Chief Kolender walking in.

I collected each officer's hours and overtime and figured out what the city owed us and submitted it to my attorney. Subsequently, we heard back from the city indicating we won our grievance. In September of 1981, we were given our back pay as an exceptional merit raise. Apparently, they can take your pay away but encounter problems giving it back. Going forward, we were paid appropriately. I didn't file the grievance just for myself. I did it because it was right and just.

We didn't want additional money from the city, we only wanted what we were owed.

I'm sure wrists were slapped, and people had to admit they were wrong. At this time, looking back, I stepped on the toes of higher ups and embarrassed others to the point where I won a small battle, but began losing the war. This is where I first had a target on my back and was remembered.

CHAPTER THREE

THE RIDE-A-LONG

I WAS BEING GRILLED like a cheap steak. I knew he was after my hide. I was home on injury leave in March of 1981, when I got a phone call from Sergeant Ed Sammons. He was a burglary Sergeant from my division and said he needed to discuss a complaint and I was at the center of it.

Sammons stated, "It would behoove your career if you came to the station now!"

I replied, "I'm on injury leave with a herniated disk and in extreme pain. I'm having difficulty walking and I'm on muscle relaxers and pain killers."

He repeated more emphatically, "It would behoove your career if you came to the station NOW!!"

I asked what the complaint was about.

He refused to discuss the matter on the phone.

I was in agonizing pain, but he scared me. If I got dressed and drove the 18 miles to Northern Division, I wouldn't be able to take my pain medicine. I told Sammons, "I'm not moving too fast, Sergeant. It'll be a while before I can get there."

He replied, "I'll be here waiting."

Once off the phone, I tried to sort out what Sammons could possibly be investigating. I'd done nothing, yet what did it concern? I called a squad member, Felix Zavala, the senior man on the squad south of the freeway and a prominent character featured in retired Los Angeles Police Department Sergeant Joseph Wambaugh's book, *Lines and Shadows.*

I told him about Sammons' phone call.

He replied, "Call Castle."

Dick Castle was a Police Officer Association attorney. So, I called Castle's office and spoke to him.

Castle instructed me to answer all questions truthfully. If I felt I needed representation, call him back. I couldn't get to the station fast enough. I had to find out what this was about. But before I share Sammons beef, I need to backtrack.

While on probation, there are two ways an officer can impress his evaluating Sergeant. One is by conducting Community Alert meetings with citizens who live on his beat. The other is to take citizens on a department sponsored "ride-a-long."

In March of 1981, I was assigned north of the freeway in a San Diego community called Kearny Mesa. Except for six residential streets, it was a commercial area. On the graveyard shift, most radio calls are for burglar alarms. Most of these calls are either accidental or an employee sets off an alarm when entering the business.

One evening, I came to lineup and was asked by acting Sergeant Joe Molinoski, if I would work south of the freeway because they were one officer short.

I was elated. I loved working south of the freeway. It was where the action was and my old stomping grounds. I worked there as a reserve officer and during one of my phases after the academy. It was also my first assignment after phase training.

During my evening shift, I stopped off at a 7-Eleven® store at Central and University for a cup of coffee. As I entered the store, I noticed a college-aged young man working behind the counter talking with two young women.

The clerk looked at me and asked, "How's your evening?"

I replied, "Not too bad." I immediately sensed my presence in the store interrupted their conversation. Their attention was directed at me and the subject was now about police. As I approached the counter with my coffee cup, I asked the three, "Have any of you ever thought about becoming a police officer?"

One of the two young women said she was interested in becoming a cop and would like to work in vice.

I chuckled and replied, "Well, you have to crawl before you walk." I explained you start as a uniformed police officer, do well in the field, get recommendations from your supervisors and after four to five years you can put in for the position and be considered to become a detective. I asked her, "Have you ever gone on a citizen ride-a-long?"

She replied, "No."

I figured this was a natural and I'd make a few points with my Sergeant. I asked her if she'd like to go on a ride-a-long.

She said, "Sure."

I told her I'd need to get permission from my Sergeant. James Carver was a former Phoenix police officer and I worked with him while I was a reserve officer. He was also my Sergeant as a sworn officer. I got him on the radio and asked if he'd meet me in the parking lot at Jack Murphy Stadium a few miles away.

I told her it would take about 15 minutes and asked if she'd still be there.

She agreed to stay at the 7-Eleven® until I returned.

At the stadium, Carver smiled and said, "Great! Remember to fill out the waiver form." *

I figured I'd schedule the ride-a-long for when I returned from my day off and asked Carver to arrange for me to work south of the freeway so I could show the citizen more activity.

Carver said he'd arrange it.

I drove back to the 7-Eleven® and told her it was all set. I asked for her address to pick her up.

She asked me to pick her up at the store.

"No problem," I replied.

Little did I know she was arrested for prostitution during my two days off. She managed to bail herself out just in time for the ride-a-long.

After my days off I got a waiver form, filled it out and gave it to Sergeant Jim Barker, the Supervisor working south of the freeway. He was my first Supervisor when I was released from training. He seemed like a good guy. He told me to contact Communications and advise them I'd have a ride-a-long. I called Communications and said, "This is 312-John Avrech, I have a ride-a-long with me tonight."

Once I cleared the station, I headed for the 7-Eleven® store. She walked out of the store with a smile and told me her name was Donna.

I let her in my car and showed her how to use the radio in case I needed help and couldn't get to it.

Just as we were pulling away, I got the first call of the evening. A "hot prowl" just occurred on an adjoining beat. A hot prowl is a burglary where the offender enters a building or residence while the occupants are inside. This can be terrifying for a victim. We pulled up at the scene while other units in the area searched for the suspect. I calmed down the victim who was hysterical and gathered information for the report. I dusted for fingerprints and interviewed possible witnesses.

I tried to balance out the evening by doing a little of everything including ticket writing, parking citations, citizen contacts, field interrogations and arrests. I took radio calls and covered other officers on calls.

When things calmed down, I requested a Code-7, a lunch break and gave my location. We stopped at the Taco King on El Cajon Boulevard at Cherokee. The restaurant is well-lit and has a large glass window where you can see all the activity in the dining area from the parking lot. As we ate, I caught up on my reports. I asked Donna, "Where are you from? You sound like you're from back east."

She told me she was from Philadelphia.

I told her I'd never been to Philly. In fact, the only thing I knew about the city was the Phillies baseball team and hoagie sandwiches wrapped in newspaper. During this time several squad cars pulled up and the officers sat in their cars but didn't enter the restaurant. They kept pulling in, watched for a while and finally left. I thought maybe they were checking to see if my ride-a-long was attractive.

We finished up and I asked her if she enjoyed the ride-a-long.

She nodded yes. While driving back to the 7-Eleven®, she told me she was having a problem she'd like to discuss with me after my shift.

I said, "Okay, I'll meet you back at the store."

When I got back to the station nothing was said about my ride-a-long. It took longer than I expected to finish up my shift. Finally, back at the 7-Eleven®, the clerk advised me Donna waited and I just missed her. The address she gave me for the waiver was 4050 Menlo Avenue, a few blocks away. I drove there and saw she was just pulling up and still in her car.

I apologized for making her wait and asked if she still wanted to talk.

Yes, she did.

I suggested we go for coffee.

She replied she'd rather stay close by. She parked her car and got in my car.

I started driving, not knowing where to go. I decided to drive to a church parking lot at 52nd and Orange. Our units used the lot to fill out reports and arrange meets with other units. Because it was on a hill, you could see several streets in the area. I turned to her and said, "What's up?"

She started telling me the difficulty she was having meeting new people. She revealed she had few friends and burst into tears.

I replied maybe she was going about it the wrong way. I reassured her; things would turn around. There were clubs, churches, libraries and the beach where she could meet people. Being a softy for feminine tears, I gave her a chaste kiss on the forehead.

She didn't go into any more detail but asked me If I'd drive her back to her apartment.

I dropped her off, wished her luck and drove home.

A few days later I was at home. While in the bathroom I stood up from the toilet and felt a stabbing pain and fell to the cold, tile floor.

I tried to get up, wincing in pain, but couldn't walk. I crawled on the floor to the bedroom and called my wife, Susan. She came home from work and helped me get dressed so I could go to the emergency room at Kaiser Hospital. I was diagnosed with a herniated disk and was in excruciating pain. I injured myself back in high school lifting heavy weights and the doctor told me it was probably where my pain stemmed from. I could handle a lot of pain but, I never experienced pain like this before. I was prescribed powerful drugs for pain and muscle spasms. They didn't even put a dent in the searing pain.

I notified the department of my disc injury and was placed on disability for six weeks.

I worried, this could finish my career as a cop, right here and now. It took three solid weeks for the pain to subside.

This is when I got the call from Sergeant Sammons. What could he possibly want?

I could barely move and had no business driving, but my mind was doing mental gymnastics. If this was how an innocent person felt, I'd hate to find out what a guilty person felt. My mind ran through a gamut of emotions. It took me 25 minutes to drive to the Northern Division station.

When I arrived, I gingerly got out of my car and walked up the steps to the side door. I was in extreme pain, fearful, angry and filled with trepidation about what was on his mind. I found Sammons, a husky-built man with curly brown hair and piercing eyes, at his desk. He directed me to an interview room. He told me the complaint was about the ride-a-long.

I thought there was nothing I did on the Ride-a-Long to cause Donna to complain. Sammons continued, "One of the officers recognized her with you. He went to Sergeant Barker and asked, "How come Avrech has a hooker with him as a ride-a-long?" Barker found the ride-a-long waiver and ran her criminal history. She was a prostitute arrested just two days before.

Now, everything fell into place. All the squad cars pulled up to the taco joint without coming inside made sense. I didn't know she was a prostitute. I hadn't worked south of the freeway for six months and never ran into her before the night in question. She didn't make a complaint against me, the officers did. Even Barker and Carver didn't know she was a prostitute until it was brought to their attention. Sammons asked me:

- Did you date Donna Gentile in the sexual sense?
- Did you pay her any money?
- Did you have sex with her?
- Did you go out with her?
- Did you touch her in any way?

My answers were no, I didn't date her in the sexual sense, nor did I pay her any money. I didn't have sex with her. I did drive to a church lot to discuss her problem and I kissed her on the forehead.

Sammons questions started meandering away from the scope of the investigation into financial and personal areas. Sammons asked me what kind of car I drove?

I told him I owned two cars, a 1973 Chevrolet Caprice and a 1977 Datsun F-10.

Sammons mused, "It must take a lot of gas to fill up that Chevy."

I said, "Yes it does, why?"

"Just wondering." He followed with, "It must cost a lot of money to do that."

I said, "Yes it does, why?"

Again, he repeated, "Just wondering."

I'm capable of remaining patient and calm in most situations. However, sitting in an uncomfortable chair, in agonizing pain while wishing I was home in bed; his ridiculous questions brought me to a boiling point. I lost my temper and blurted out, "Are you trying to say I'm living beyond my means and would have to steal or do something dishonest to get by?"

Sammons said, "I didn't say that. You did."

I told Sammons he was way off-beam. I angrily said, "I did nothing wrong, so leave me the hell alone. This investigation is a farce, it's bullshit and you're a goddamn asshole!" I think the last two words cost me a written reprimand.*

Years later after he retired from the police department, I contacted Sammons at home by phone and was told he and a Northern Division secretary named Wendy Jones drove to The Hitching Post Motel on El Cajon Boulevard and interviewed Donna Gentile. The essence of the interview revealed the same answers as I gave Sammons. He apologized for being so heavy handed, but said he was just doing his job and meant no hard feelings.

Sammons told me over the phone, "Captain Ecklund really wanted your ass on this investigation."

As I left Sammons' office he said, "If we believe you, this matter won't go any further. But if we don't, I'll send it to Internal Affairs."

About a week later, while still convalescing at home, I got a knock at my front door. When I went to the door, I recognized Arthur Turman, a Sergeant working Central Division downtown. I opened the door and noticed he was wearing street clothes. I welcomed him in and asked what I could do for him.

Turman said, "I'm working vacation relief for another Sergeant in Internal Affairs and I just want to ask you some questions."

I immediately assumed the department didn't believe me and sent the matter to Internal Affairs.

Turman told me he was sent to notify me he received information from a prostitute. She told him she engaged in sex with a San Diego Police Officer and contracted a sexually transmitted disease. She wanted to notify the department so the officer could get treatment.

I thought the department didn't believe me and now they were coming up with a bullshit lie, thinking they'd scare me into admitting I lied. I asked Turman, "Why are you coming to me at home? Is this Sammons' doing?"

Turman replied no, but they were aware of the investigation. He stated the girl identified herself only by the first name "Cheryl." She described the officer "to a T" and I fit the description, so I must be the officer.

I started to do a slow burn. I told Turman, "I don't associate with prostitutes, I don't know anyone with the first name Cheryl, and I wasn't the officer in question. You're wasting your time coming to me at my house."

After he left, I sat on the living room floor, shaking my head. I thought, this is the San Diego P.D. "America's Finest City" and supposedly the best place in the country to be a cop. All I could do was wonder.

I never heard from Turman or Internal Affairs again. However, years later I discovered "Cheryl" was referring to another officer.

I got a written reprimand for violating the ride-a-long policy, for not having the citizen write down their comments on the reverse side of the waiver form. The reprimand stayed in my file for one year. It was mentioned in my evaluation the next month. It was also mentioned in my six-month evaluation and my annual evaluation. It prevented me from getting choice assignments, training schools or specialized training

After this incident, I received ongoing snide remarks from Lieutenant Jim Sing. When it happened, Sing was the Investigative Lieutenant under Captain Carl Ecklund. One day while I was working light duty until my back injury fully healed, he passed my desk and said, "Hey Avrech, we choked your girlfriend out the other night."

Apparently, she was arrested again and this time resisted arrest. The officers used a carotid restraint hold, known as a sleeper hold, to restrain her. Sing's remarks were unprofessional and unnecessary. Apparently, the department couldn't handle the fact I was innocent of any wrongdoing. But they needed to give me something, so it was a note in my file for not having her write down notes about what she experienced on the ride-a-long.

CHAPTER FOUR

WAITING FOR THE OTHER SHOE
TO DROP

It was stressful enough coming to work to dispense a little justice and make it home alive, just to do it all over again the next day. It was a jungle out there, fighting with a suspect on PCP in the middle of traffic on busy El Cajon Boulevard. A 135-pound male "whacked out" on Angel Dust sweating profusely and with his adrenaline kicked up, he possessed the strength of ten men. I was worried about myself, my cover officer, the suspect, traffic on both sides of the street and making sure he didn't reach for my gun or my cover officer's gun.

At the time all you could use against a threat such as this was sheer body weight. Police approved sleeper holds were no match for this phenomenon. You could render the subject unconscious for several seconds. But, he'd regain consciousness and fight all over again. This occurred to me and my cover officer Gib Ninness one evening. Before other cover units could arrive, it required the assistance of a citizen riding a bicycle who stopped to help. Once the person was subdued, we took him to County Mental Health (C.M.H.) where it took three shots of "Haldol®" a powerful antipsychotic drug to control him.

Looking back, I knew my career was advancing at a snail's pace. I was turned down for assignments to work active areas so to increase my chances for promotion to detective. After being deployed north of the freeway in a less productive area of the city, I was transferred to "C" squad which operated from 7:00pm to 3:00am. It was the shift where you could attend school if you were studying for a degree and still make time to sleep and study prior to your shift.

I was working for Sergeant Pat McLarney, who recently worked as a Burglary Detective before being promoted. The general progression was usually from uniformed patrol to detective, if promoted to Sergeant you went back to uniformed patrol and back to detective as a plain clothes detective Sergeant. McLarney enjoyed having me work for him as I'd complete follow-up in the field normally left unfinished on most reports he received. It required him to do the follow-ups on most of his cases. But he found mine were always complete. As a new law regarding Felony Spouse Beating was added to the penal codes in 1982, there came a chance to use this in the field. I responded to such a call on another officer's beat.

Pat looked at me and said, "Larry, I know this isn't your beat, but I know you'll do a better job. Would you take the case and arrest report for me?" *

I did without hesitation. Even though I was moved to another watch after my three-month stint with him, I received a better evaluation from him as opposed to others. It was purely based on performance as opposed to hearsay and innuendo. I thought maybe my career chances were improving.

In 1983, I wrote an arrest report for a *DUI/Hit and Run sent back to my command as an exemplary report. I understand it was used at the academy for training purposes through 1991, although my name was redacted after I left the department.

I was holding my own one day in 1983, when Rich Draper came to Eastern Division on a disciplinary transfer from another. He was the source of several complaints involving excessive force both on and off duty. I was asked to secretly evaluate him.

Why ask me? Because Carl Black was my Lieutenant now. The jury was still out on him, but I didn't like what I was hearing and seeing.

I was working for Sergeant Bob Rex. I thought to myself, now I'll be working in the same car with a troublemaker and if one of us gets in trouble, both of us will take the fall. In this way, Black could kill two birds with one stone.

It was a relatively quiet night, we wrote a couple of Field Interrogations, a couple of tickets and now we received a radio call to handle a disturbance, where we encountered a person who was intoxicated in public.

San Diego used a Detox facility where cooperative people could be taken to sober up. It was an alternative to being booked into jail. If they didn't create a disturbance or try to leave the facility for four hours, they were released with no other paperwork involved. There were mats on the floor to sleep on, you could sit and play cards or walk around until your four-hour time limit was up. If you created a disturbance after being dropped off, we'd receive a call back and now the person was a detox reject and booked into jail.

This night we picked up a cooperative drunk and transported him to Detox. While I was signing him in, Draper got out of the unit to contact a citizen outside the facility. I was oblivious to the conversation. A few minutes later, I started walking out of the facility back to my unit, when I noticed Draper saying goodbye to the citizen and walking back to our unit. I got into my squad car at the same time as Draper. My driver's side window was down a crack. I looked at Draper and said, "What did the citizen want?"

Draper turned to me and waved me off with his hand saying, "Never mind, I'll tell you later, it was no big deal."

I started pulling into the street and heard the man utter the word, "Number."

I hit the brakes and said to Draper, "Is he talking to us?"

Draper replied, "No! never mind, I already told him what to do."

We left the downtown area, hit the freeway and returned to our area. Once there, about 20 minutes later, Communications called our unit with a message, 312 King 10-21 the Watch Commander.

I turned to Draper and said, "Rich what did you do! You'd better tell me now! I need to know!" I felt they knew Draper would foul up and get me at the same time. Otherwise, he could've ridden with a supervisor or a more senior officer. There was a method to his madness. Bob Rex was a good supervisor and always backed up his troops.

After talking with the Watch Commander, I learned the citizen at Detox was creating a disturbance because his lady friend was taken there. He felt she wouldn't be safe dressed to the nines wearing expensive jewelry.

The people running detox told the man she'd be safe and he was required to leave the property and wait for her to be released. Prior to our arrival, a female officer dropping someone off explained the man could wait on the sidewalk outside, contrary to what the Detox employees said. The female officer left, and he was standing on the sidewalk outside the door. Apparently, he was told again by the staff to move away from the door and was walking away as we drove up. We never found out who the female officer was, but Draper was telling the man the female officer was incorrect and he was to move away. Confused the man said, "Look, you tell me one thing; the detox people tell me another and the female officer tells me something else, I want a supervisor."

Draper retorted angrily, "You don't rate a supervisor!"

His remark was the reason the citizen phoned in a complaint. To top it off as we were leaving, I heard the man utter the word, "Number." He was asking for Draper's badge number. So, Draper was rude to a citizen and failed to give him his badge number.

I discussed this with Bob Rex. He believed what I relayed to him was all Draper's doing. Rex said, "But it's not up to me, it'll be up to Lieutenant Black to decide." He asked Draper and I to write officers reports on the incident.*

Everything on Draper's report was accurate except he omitted the fact he was rude to the citizen and refused to provide him with his badge number.

The incident occurred on August 18, 1983 and I didn't hear about it for two weeks. After lineup, I was asked to step into Lieutenant Black's office.

With a big grin on his face, Black asked me if I'd relate to him what occurred at Detox. When I was finished, I noticed a piece of paper, blank side up on his desk.

He starred at me for a few seconds, looking me square in the face and called me a liar. Black claimed I lied to protect myself and both of us, "would swing for it." Black turned the paper over and asked me to read the written warning.

As I was reading the reprimand Black stated, "I think you lied, but I'm going to give you the benefit of the doubt. I knew this would go further if I refused to sign, so I signed it and left the room. Now there was another piece of paper in my file to further stagnate my career chances.

Black went on to tell supervision and others at Eastern Division I was a liar. In a private conversation, Black confided with Sergeant Connie Zimmerman, who became one of my Sergeants at Eastern later in the year. Black made the statement, "As far as Larry Avrech's career is concerned, it's over!"

When Zimmerman told me this, I knew he was after me. Early on, Zimmerman and Black were in a relationship before my time. But when all this trouble started, she sided with me, because she knew I always told the truth. She was aware of his past and we continue to be friends to this day. This would be the basis for my investigation of him and a prostitute almost a year later. He would be a hypocrite of his own policies for being honest and truthful when he got involved with Donna Gentile.

CHAPTER FIVE

MY INVESTIGATION

I DROVE a four and a half mile stretch of El Cajon Boulevard once from where it starts in San Diego to the La Mesa city limit. I counted over 110 prostitutes, sometimes as many as ten on one street corner. Business owners complained their presence was bad for business. Used condoms and syringes were found strewn all over the area. Something had to be done.

My Lieutenant, Carlton F. Black was the Eastern Division Patrol Lieutenant chosen by the department to command the Prostitution Enforcement detail. Prostitution was out of control in San Diego in 1984. It was up to Eastern Division to devise a plan to handle the problem.

On that stretch of road, the heaviest concentration of prostitutes was at Felton Street and El Cajon Boulevard where a 7-Eleven® convenience store was located. They would get a cheap bite to eat, get off the street, buy condoms or use the pay phones to communicate with their "Johns" or pimps.

Between this location and the La Mesa city limits were liquor stores, fast food restaurants, cheap motels used as "trick pads," cabbie stands, banks with ATM machines and more convenience stores. At 52nd and 70th Street, Donna Gentile frequented the corner along with other prostitutes. Next door to the 7-Eleven® was a laundromat where Gentile did her laundry. Two blocks east, a Pacific Bell building stood, where she sat on a bus bench and plied her trade.

San Diego developed a plan like the successful one adopted by the City of San Jose. This included "selective enforcement." So if a prostitute was stopped and while speaking with an officer she dropped or threw her cigarette away; she'd be cited for littering. Or, she'd be written up for throwing a lit projectile in the street. If she was stopped for a traffic violation and found to have a warrant, she'd be arrested and taken off the street. Any equipment violations were subject to citation. If a parked vehicle was more than 18 inches from the curb, we'd cite them. If a girl was on a street corner, we'd pull up with our blue overhead lights flashing. No "John" in his right mind would stop and engage in conversation while we were there. If a girl got in a vehicle we'd follow behind the car. The John would get spooked and let her out. Or, if he had any equipment violations, we'd pull him over and speak to both of them. We'd collect their information and take appropriate action. We were instructed to offer the girls a cab to pick them up if they wanted one. If they got in their own car, we'd follow it until it left the boulevard. Some went home for the night. Others went downtown, or, to the naval bases where Vice units worked their own detail. Some even got fed up and left town.

During this detail, I stopped a prostitute talking with a John. I recognized him as my wife's former fiancé from before we met. She dumped him several years ago and I found it amusing he was talking to a prostitute. In conversations, he always told her he'd never pay for sex when he could get it free. After collecting his information, he got in his car and took off.

I turned to Gentile and asked, "What's his trip?"

"Oh, he's a trick," she said confirming my suspicion.

I asked her to show me a driver's license or ID card.

As she produced a valid California Driver's License she mentioned, "I won't be hassled much longer. I got a Lieutenant in my hip pocket."

I replied, "What! You're screwing one of the brass?"

She said, "I'll tell you if you come to my apartment after work." She lived in La Mesa just outside the San Diego city limits.

After my shift, I went to her apartment in a shabby complex to find out who she was talking about. If this was a bunch of bull, I would've dropped it and told others she was a liar and to be leery of her. However, if it was true, I needed as much information as possible so I could turn it over to Internal Affairs. I arrived at her apartment located at 4341 Spring St #47 at the Spring Hill Apartments in La Mesa close to El Cajon Boulevard.

When she opened the door, she was wearing a sheer, red teddy. As she stood in the doorway, I looked past her to a wall and saw a San Diego Sheriff's Department decal about two feet in diameter which normally adorns the door of squad vehicles. "Come in," she invited me.

"No, I'll stand in the doorway," I replied. It became a cat and mouse game and I figured I was wasting time. This was a stalemate and I wouldn't compromise myself.

She stood there silent; her nipples barely shrouded in the sheer red fabric. She was "loaded for bear" waiting for me to be tempted.

However, I was smarter than the average bear. Again, I refused to be compromised. It simply wasn't in my moral fiber. Instead of getting turned on, I was getting pissed off. I angrily told her, "Look, either you tell me who you're talking about, or I'm outta here!"

I began walking down the stairs when she finally blurted out, "It's Carl!"

I turned and asked, "Carl who? There are a lot of 'Carls' in the Department."

With irritation in her voice she said, "It's Carl Black!"

"I don't believe you," I shot back.

She insisted, "I'm telling you the truth."

I asked for her phone number so I could communicate with her, instead of driving the streets looking for her.

I kept thinking about what she said as I drove home. Was my Lieutenant dirty? Was he extending her courtesy or favors? How could he be involved? I needed to learn more.

I had a follow-up phone conversation with her the next day. Still in disbelief, Gentile revealed she was going to the Colorado River next weekend with Black, other members of the department and their spouses.

I called Connie Zimmerman, one of my Sergeants who was on leave of absence studying for the California State Bar. After sharing with her what I learned, she gave me some direction.

If I made an uncorroborated statement against an officer, I could ruin his career and possibly lose my job. She suggested I sit on the information until it could be verified and brought forward. I had nowhere else to go. I couldn't go to my Sergeant (Goudarzi), he was working the detail with Black and frequently rode with him. He might be involved, which is why I told Zimmerman. She was neutral and I trusted her.

Over the weekend, I checked the computer for tickets, arrests or Field Interrogation slips to see if Gentile was in the system. She wasn't spotted on "the Boulevard" anywhere and calls to her apartment went unanswered. The next time I reached her was June 28th. In a phone conversation she described the fun she had the weekend before at the Colorado River.

I asked her who showed up?

She told, me two Sergeant's from Southeast Division, one was named Ken and the other she couldn't remember. His wife Ginny was loud, boisterous and kept flashing her tits, she said. Based on her description, I knew both her and her husband.

I previously worked for the Campus Police at University of San Diego with Jeff Fellows and his wife, Virginia. The other Sergeant was Ken Hargrove. He and Black were old friends and worked together years ago.

I asked Gentile, "Who did you sleep with?"

She stated, she was set up with Hargrove and had sex with him at the river.

"Did you take any pictures?" I asked.

Carl was developing the film and she'd have them later in the week.*

I told her, "I'd sure like to see them."

Gentile stated she camped at Martinez Lake in Martinez, Arizona along the Colorado River. It was about 35 miles from Yuma. She cut her foot while there and Black took her to a Yuma medical center. She used an alias and he paid for her foot to be stitched up. She told me she needed to do laundry and would be at the laundromat in the evening with a bandaged foot.

After hanging up the phone I thought my God, what a hypocrite.

When Lieutenant Carl Black first came to Eastern Division, he joined one of our lineup meetings and introduced himself. But instead of saying if we had any questions or concerns, his door was always open; he gave us a totally different message. "If there's anything I can't stand its dishonesty or a liar. If you ever lie to me, I'll have you fired!" he barked.

So, my Lieutenant who demanded honesty. took a prostitute to the Colorado River, procuring him for a Sergeant friend. He also allowed her to give false information at a medical facility. I don't know who suggested it. Obviously, Gentile didn't want medical information traced back to her or to Black, since he was responsible and paid for her foot to be stitched up.

On June 29th I drove to the laundromat at 70th and El Cajon. Her car was parked out front. I went in and immediately noticed a large gauze bandage on her foot. While there, I monitored radio calls in case I was called, or if another unit needed assistance.

Gentile told me Black gave her five hundred dollars on two separate occasions. He also co-signed for her bail when she was arrested. I'd just heard a mouthful.

Just then my Sergeant pulled up and motioned to me. I walked out, and he said, "Be careful of her, she's trouble." I needed to get the pictures from their weekend fun before I could move forward. Words mean little, but a picture paints a thousand words.

I never got hold of the pictures or I would've kept them and gone to Internal Affairs. Realizing she couldn't compromise me after numerous offers of sex, she understood I gave her nothing in return. She was doing all the talking which swept away any "Sugar Daddy" excuses. She still went to Internal Affairs with trumped up allegations after talking with Sergeant Goudarzi and told him I was a dirty cop.

I was investigated by Internal Affairs and they returned with a "he said - she said" conclusion and sent it to my division.* That's where the trouble started.

I'd since moved to another watch and worked for Junior Sergeant Reggie Frank. He should've done the reinvestigation, but apparently, I became expendable. They gave the Investigation to Lieutenant William Skinner who was supposed to be more familiar with vice investigations. Four allegations suddenly multiplied into twelve and I was terminated. I immediately requested a Civil Service hearing and asked to be reinstated.

CHAPTER SIX

DONNA AND INTERNAL AFFAIRS

GENTILE WAS clever and cunning like a fox. On the exterior she gave the appearance of a normal red-blooded American woman trying to get ahead in the world. She may have dropped out of school when she first came to San Diego, but she quickly learned street skills. She had to be a negotiator when dealing with "Johns" on the street. After being arrested several times, she figured ways to minimize her exposure time in jail by having cops and others under her control. I'm sure she was schooled quickly by other street workers.

In early July of 1984, after several attempts trying to get me between the sheets didn't work, she came up with the idea of having me write a character letter to her probation officer handling her case.*

Now what was I going to do? At first, I said no and resisted her request. I had to stall for time and give her what she asked for, but I was going to do it my way. I was waiting for her to show me the pictures of the river trip, so I could snatch them from her and go forward to Internal Affairs.

Gentile told me, "You don't want to piss me off, I'll turn you in."

I asked, "For what?"

Gentile said, "Don't you worry. I'll think of something. I've turned others in before."

I came up with the idea of writing it on the cardboard backing to one of my crime /incident report forms. * It wasn't official department letterhead and I purposefully omitted the date in two places. I knew this would be questioned in court and, if I was called in to testify, I'd expose her in open court. I knew it was as worthless as if it was written on toilet paper. I felt by revealing what I exposed, it would've been to a higher authority outside the department.

I didn't trust my command and had little faith in Internal Affairs. Their job was to protect the good name of the department. If it meant withholding evidence, lying or concealing the truth, that was their purpose. Internal Affairs isn't a friend you can trust My case is living proof.

Gentile didn't accept the letter on cardboard and asked me to rewrite it on a piece of paper she provided me with.

Again, I left items omitted from this letter as well.*

To further shore up her chances in court, Gentile also asked me to contact her probation officer, Marie Bergenbach by phone since Black would also call her.

In my conversation with Bergenbach, I mentioned Black would be calling her as well to put his name out there in case Gentile was lying. Or, in the event, he got cold feet and changed his mind about calling. In this way, another agency had knowledge of the investigation outside of the department.

To my way of thinking, this gave me more time to get my hands on the incriminating river photos in her possession. Sadly, I never got my hands on them. Once Gentile realized she was in jeopardy of losing her money connection with Black if I turned him in, she had no other choice but to stop me. But, she had to wait until after her probation hearing to do so. Reports from Internal Affairs dated September 17, 1984 show Breitenstein did a phone interview with Bergenbach. We only have what Breitenstein says Bergenbach said. There's no taped interview. Thus, no one knows what she said, only what Breitenstein claims she said.

In a phone interview of Bergenbach by my Eastern Division Captain Tom Hall on December 13, 1984, Bergenbach told Hall I never recommended work furlough for Gentile as was previously alleged. I only inquired and recommended nothing less than incarceration.

Going back to August 21, 1984 I received a call to report to Internal Affairs at 10:00 a.m. the following morning.

I called Gentile knowing something was up and asked, "You wouldn't happen to know why I have to report to Internal Affairs would you?"

Gentile lied of course and replied, "No I wouldn't know about that."

I knew I had no choice but to bring everything forward at this time regarding Black and their trip to the Colorado River, photos or not.

After driving downtown to Central Headquarters, I waited for Sgt. Breitenstein. While I stood in front of his desk, I read a note on his ink blotter with Donna Gentile's name and an earlier time written for an appointment the same morning. So, I knew Gentile lied to me and only reconfirmed my suspicions.

Once inside the interview room, I was joined by Sergeant Bill Pfahler and Sergeant Glenn Breitenstein. I didn't have counsel with me at the time. They advised me the proceeding was administrative in nature and not a criminal matter. Then they informed me of the charges. They claimed:

- I had sexual intercourse with Gentile while on duty. (She said, she'd think up something.)
- I provided her with information of a restricted nature regarding police files.
- Association with a known prostitute under police investigation.
- I solicited Gentile to make a false complaint against another officer.

Before I left, I was asked if I had any questions. This is when I informed them of what my investigation revealed. I got bewildered looks from Breitenstein, but I went on and told him while glancing at the tape recorder to make sure the tape wasn't running out. I wanted them to capture the entire incident on tape as I saw it unravel.

Breitenstein asked me to explain the detail to him and what our assignment was while dealing with the prostitutes on the Boulevard. We were under orders to use selective enforcement when dealing with them. If they were smoking and threw their cigarette in the street, we were to cite them or pull over if they were attempting to hail drivers to ply their trade. We would pull over with our overhead lights on until they left the area. If they wanted a cab, we would call a cab and make sure they left the area. Or, if they played cat and mouse games with us, we'd follow them off the Boulevard. Gentile played games with the officers and drove around in circles. It was a game to her and we'd waste precious time on the street, but those were our orders. I personally relieved an officer who got tired of driving around the block 27 times.*

During this time, I wasn't aware my Reserve partner was called in and interviewed the previous day. Afterwards, I learned they pulled him in and questioned him regarding me as it related to Gentile. He told them at the time he heard a rumor about Carl Black taking Gentile to the Colorado River with other officers.

I told Breitenstein everything I knew about the river trip, the money Black gave her, the other officers and their wives and Gentile cutting her foot at the river and having my Lieutenant pay for medical attention.

The interview was stopped until August 27 at 3:00 pm when we continued with counsel.

I didn't care for the looks I was getting.

On August 27, at 2:58 pm, we continued the interview. I was informed there was an additional allegation added against me: that I observed Gentile commit a criminal act and failed to take enforcement action. In Breitenstein's words he said, "This is an additional allegation that's come to light since we last discussed this incident."

While the "Bully Boys" were brow-beating me, my P.O.A. (Police Officers Association) assigned attorney, Edward Dillon sat there like a statue and uttered only a few words.*

"Can I ask a question?"

"Is the coffee ready?"

"Thank you."

"Is this a hearing or a question and answer period?"

I could have done much better without counsel. Is this what I paid my association dues every month for? They wanted to add yet another allegation: I owned a comic book business without approval from the department. A Sergeant friend who was a liaison officer to the City Attorney's Office told me as long as I didn't call in sick because of the extra hours and as long as it didn't create any conflict of interest or was a police-regulated business, it was okay. Breitenstein himself owned a construction company.

During the taped interview we discussed the allegations in depth. After 90 minutes we concluded the interview.

On September 26, I received a memo from Internal Affairs* stating the investigation into the Gentile investigation was finished and the results would be sent to my command. The results of their investigation were as follows:

1. Associating with a known prostitute under criminal investigation. (Sustained)
2. Provided restricted information from police files. (Running two license plates Internal Affairs gave Gentile to entrap me.) (Sustained)
3. Neglected Duty/ Sex on Duty. (Not Sustained)
4. Observed a criminal act and failed to take enforcement action. (Not Sustained)
5. Solicited Gentile to make a false complaint against another officer. (Not Sustained)

When I saw the results I thought, I had to associate with her in order to get information regarding her relationship with Lieutenant Black. I wasn't concerned about their findings. I could explain it easily if the matter went any further.

Providing license plate information was commonplace for one and for a dollar you could get the information if you stood in line at the Department of Motor Vehicles. As a Private Investigator, most P.I.'s were ex-cops. They would call one of their buddies or contacts to run criminal histories, plates or warrants or a multitude of other things. Only information pertaining to one plate was given to her. Internal Affairs thought they'd throw me a curve. One of the plates they gave Gentile for me to run was for a vice vehicle.* I recalled the tag number when she gave it to me. When it came back as not on file it confirmed my suspicions. I refused to provide any information regarding the vehicle. I wasn't going to burn an undercover vehicle. Internal Affairs didn't think I'd recognize the plate when they gave it to her.

During this time, unbeknownst to me, Internal Affairs was camped out at her apartment and were providing scripts for Gentile. There would be long pauses to my questions and Gentile was a liar, but not a good one.

Neglecting my Duty and having sex on duty was an allegation they changed. They said by associating with her, I was neglecting my duty which should've been in the first allegation of my association. Nevertheless, the allegation wasn't sustained. The sex on duty charge should've been unfounded altogether. I will explain more later.

The charge of observing Gentile commit an act of prostitution and taking no enforcement action wasn't sustained. My partner and I followed her to an apartment building. She went inside before my partner could park and we couldn't see or hear anything. She was inside for 20 minutes or so and when she came outside, we followed her off the boulevard. This should've been unfounded as well.

The final allegation about asking Gentile to file a complaint against another officer was also not sustained.

I felt the two sustained allegations could be explained away and I'd just move on. I hoped they'd take appropriate action against Carl Black, but he had Godfather's on the department and knew things about higher ups. I didn't have the same knowledge.

So, why should the sex on duty charge have been completely unfounded? When you lie, you need to remember two things: First you need to remember what you said, "forever." The second is if you lie, you better know the subject matter you're lying about.

Prior to going into custody, Gentile made a tape recording which was given to her attorney Douglas Holbrook. It stated, "In case I disappear somewhere or am missing, I want my lawyer to give this to the press. I have no intention of disappearing or going out of town without letting my lawyer know first. Because of the publicity that I have given a police scandal, this is the reason why I am making this...I feel someone in a uniform with a badge can still be a serious criminal."

When Gentile went into custody, she did a phone interview from jail and told a reporter I first contacted her three and a half years ago when I took her on a ride-a-long.

Gentile told the reporter in June of 1984, when I was working "backup" to an undercover operation, I pulled up in an unmarked police vehicle and said, "Hey remember me?" and told her to get in the vehicle because it would go easier on her. Then, I drove to a location and had sex with her.

In June of 1984, I was working in a regular marked unit and wasn't working backup to any Vice Operation.

What Gentile didn't realize and what my command should've realized but refused to, was for an officer to check out an undercover vehicle at Eastern Division, you must sign a clipboard in the Investigative Lieutenant's office and have him approve it. Nobody takes a car without authorization, which was a policy and procedure Gentile knew nothing about. Another allegation which should've been unfounded.

But apparently it didn't fit their agenda.

My command could've dropped the investigation or given me a reprimand for not going through channels and doing a proper investigation, but my Captain decided to make an example of me for investigating one of his officers and a higher up.

The department was given many opportunities to clear me but took no action.

Breitenstein asked Gentile if she'd take a polygraph exam. She agreed but none was given.

I would've taken one, but I was never asked. Either way, if Gentile was tested and failed, they would have no case against me. Also, if I was tested and found to be truthful, they would have no case. So, it was better for Internal Affairs to not know the truth when investigating me. The truth didn't matter, but they were perfectly willing to take the word of a liar with absolutely no credibility. I also believe Internal Affairs instilled fear in Gentile. The next night, after cooperating with Internal Affairs Investigators to tape our phone conversations, Gentile's car was broken into.

My ex-wife's perception of her conversation with Breitenstein was she should be in danger from me. She wasn't.*

Gentile's friend Cynthia Maine, another murder victim and a true informant, was afraid after she was released from jail.

It seems there's a common denominator here. Breitenstein and/or Internal Affairs planted the suggestion in Gentile's mind to make a tape in the event she suddenly disappeared. This makes more sense than two prostitutes being clairvoyants.

For example, if Gentile was really in fear as she claimed, why wasn't I taken off the streets? Why wasn't I removed from the field? It wasn't until after I was involved in an off-duty accident in October of 1984. This involved a child who rode her bicycle off the center median and collided with my vehicle in traffic.* I was shaken up by the incident and glad she wasn't seriously injured, but I still asked for half the night off. At this time I was removed from the field by Lieutenant Ron Seden. (See Patrol journals*)

Unless Goudarzi was involved in some way with Donna, I find it hard to believe a seasoned investigator like himself was unable to see through Lieutenant Black's deception.

Also, if Gentile was the "informant" she claimed to be and wrote home or called frequently, why didn't she communicate about how scary it was to do the work she was supposed to be doing for the department? Or, why did she never tell family members or friends back in Pennsylvania how much she enjoyed "the work" she was doing. It only came up when she went to jail, expecting the department to help her out and she discovered otherwise. However, there was no mention of it until then.

CHAPTER SEVEN

I TOLD THE TRUTH BUT IT WASN'T ENOUGH

On September 26, 1984, I received an interoffice memo from Internal Affairs my investigation was complete and the package would be sent to my command.*

During the first week of October 1984, my Captain, Tom Hall received the Internal Affairs report. He had the choice to forget the matter, provide disciplinary action if necessary, or continue the investigation. He decided to reinvestigate the matter and sought another Lieutenant, William Skinner, to look into the matter.

Skinner called me into his office one evening after lineup and hammered me with questions. I didn't expect this to happen, especially with no counsel present. We finally quit. I was told to obtain an attorney by the next time we met. Once I had my attorney with me, we rehashed the Internal Affairs investigation page by page for over five hours. Every time my attorney objected to Skinner's questions, he raised his voice and put him in his place. Honestly, my attorney was absolutely worthless. He might as well have not been present at all.

I was physically drained after his repeated questioning that droned on from 10:00 pm until 3:30 am. I spoke to a friend, Mike Augustin, who worked the adjoining beat with me.

Mike said, "Well if he gets on your case again, he has a sordid past of his own. Remember the countywide lockbox burglary series?"

I replied, "Yes, the burglary series that went unsolved for four years. Someone was using a Real Estate agent's key to break into houses for sale, stealing jewelry and resetting the stones."

Mike said, "You might look up Jack Duane Sargent and Melba Marie Skinner* in the computer." I received a copy of the case in the mail and obtained computer printouts on both suspects.

*Skinner was relentless in his efforts to catch me in a lie. He went over every word of the Internal Affairs tape and recorded phone conversations I had with Gentile. He asked me repeatedly, "Why did you say that? What did that mean?" The truth just wasn't good enough.

As it turned out, Skinner's ex-wife and her compatriot were the suspects in this series, and they were spotted in a vehicle seen in the area of previous burglaries. Because they were spotted in Santee outside the city limits, they were now in the Sheriff's jurisdiction. The Sheriff's department was called, the vehicle stopped and the two arrested. When they were brought to the Sheriff's substation, Skinner showed up and was asked to leave because he was interfering.

Since this was a countywide and citywide series, Skinner who was a Sergeant at the time, was in the Special Investigations unit also investigating the series. Her composite sketch* hung in his office where you'd think someone or Skinner himself would've thought, "Gee, that looks a lot like my ex-wife."

I was going to mention this next time Skinner raked me over the coals. But before I got the chance, I was suspended from using the computers. Apparently, the department knew this burglary series was a sensitive matter and didn't want others knowing. So, the department red-flagged the information in the system to notify them if anyone ran the reports.

I was called in and asked why I ran Skinner and Sargent's information.

I told them I was tired of being harassed by Skinner.

On January 15, 1985, one week before my official termination, a memo with my picture* was circulated to all department divisions by my Investigative Lieutenant, Ron Seden. It read:

To all personnel

Officer Larry Avrech ID# 2900 has been suspended from duty pending investigation effective this date. Until further notice he is under orders not to be within or on the grounds of any San Diego Police Department Facility unless escorted by an on-duty San Diego Police Department Supervisor, nor is he to be allowed entry to such facilities by anyone unless so escorted. Your cooperation is appreciated.

Cc: Central Division

Northern Division

Southeastern Division

Southern Division

Northeastern Division

Western Division

Front Counter Central

Crime Analysis

Records Division

Teletype

Traffic

The original document with my photo was also mailed to me.

Unfortunately, it didn't stop there either. I was later investigated by Internal Affairs for violating a direct order not to discuss this investigation until it was completed. I was told the investigation was complete so I saw no reason to remain silent. These allegations were added to the original Internal Affairs Investigation. Now I was fighting not four or five allegations, but twelve of them. Skinner turned this into an unwinnable case. They were as follows:

Unbecoming Conduct

Immoral Conduct

Abuse of Position

Associations

Public Statements and Appearances

Performance of Duty

Neglect of Duty

Dissemination of Information

Investigations

Truthfulness

Obedience to a Lawful Order

Informant Contacts

By the time I went to my Civil Service hearing the following May, I had all these charges stacked against me. I prevailed over five of the twelve allegations mentioned above. These included: Immoral

Conduct, Public Statements and Appearances, Truthfulness, Obedience to a Lawful Order and Informant Contacts.*

The other seven charges I failed to overcome were Unbecoming Conduct, Abuse of Position, Associations, Performance of Duty, Neglect of Duty, Dissemination of Information and Investigations.*

As you can see, I told the truth, but it wasn't enough. This investigation had absolutely nothing to do with telling the truth. More pointedly, it was about image and what the public is made to think about a police department of a major American city. When it came down to one or the other, the department will always side with keeping up their appearances and image.

CHAPTER EIGHT

DIRTY TRICKS

"So, you want to be a regular officer, huh?" Sergeant Larry Moratto said, as my Reserve partner, Steve Tompkins was threatened and intimidated by Internal Affairs Sergeant's Moratto and Glenn Breitenstein. Of course, you won't find it anywhere on his recorded interview,* as these questions were barked at Tomkins before the tape recorder was turned on.

Internal Affairs was looking for anything Tompkins possibly saw or heard to corroborate any of Donna Gentile's allegations brought against me.

I took Steve under my wing shortly after he graduated from the Reserve Academy.

A lot of sworn officers he rode with didn't like the Reserves. Their attitude was, "Hey look, I didn't ask for you, so don't touch the radio, write the journal and keep your mouth shut. It's bad enough I have to worry about my own ass and not coming home in one piece, now I have to worry about you screwing up and getting me killed."

Fortunately, I accepted Steve. I trained him properly and taught him everything I knew. He was one of the first Reserve Training Officers sent to the Academy as an advisor. We worked together two or three nights a week for about three years.

People in the squad referred to us as the odd couple, like actors Tony Randall and Jack Klugman from the popular TV show back in the day.

When I left the field, he was more competent than some sworn officers and he continued the force for 34 years before recently stepping down.

Both Internal Affairs Sergeant's Breitenstein and Moratto hammered Tompkins about an accusation Gentile made. It was an incident where we followed her to an apartment off Wabash and University. She entered an apartment and was inside for 20 to 25 minutes. Apparently, she could see our silhouettes from inside, but at night we couldn't see her inside. Her allegation was she was committing an act of prostitution and we did nothing to stop the crime.

Most assuredly, if I knew a crime was being committed in my presence, I would always take appropriate action.

Although, we could make an educated guess as to what was happening inside, probable cause is formed by first-hand knowledge, using all your senses and/or by a corroborating witness. So, barring that, we stood our ground and followed orders continuing to follow her until she left the streets.

Other questions were asked of Tompkins regarding the amount of time I spent upstairs at Gentile's apartment. Tompkins, concerned for my safety, followed me upstairs minutes later to find me standing outside her apartment door.

When Tompkins was asked to come to Internal Affairs on August 21, 1984 he was off duty. The interview took place at 3:21 pm. This is the essence of his interview.

Breitenstein: "Okay. Uh, I'm ordering you to answer the following questions."

Tompkins: "Isn't that, isn't that for regulars?"

Breitenstein: "Uh, it also applies to you as a reserve."

Tompkins: "Oh, it, why? Am I on duty or something?"

Moratto: "No, all, all the regulations of our department, while you're working as a police officer."

Tompkins: "Yeah, when I'm on duty."

Moratto: "Okay, you come under the constraints of those and anything that we do. For instance if we wanted, if we want to terminate you out of the reserve program, that's an administrative procedure."

Once Steve understood where the two bullyboys were coming from, he cooperated with them and answered their questions. Unfortunately, they didn't like the truth because they were unable to verify any of Gentile's allegations against me.

Breitenstein showed Tompkins a picture of Donna Gentile and asked him if he could identify her.

Tompkins stated the following: "Yeah."

Breitenstein: "How do you know this individual?"

Tompkins: "Uh, cause she's a prostitute that frequents El Cajon Boulevard and she's probably been the single sole problem up on El Cajon Boulevard to the whole detail. The one who kept coming backout and uh, we'd have to follow her around on the streets and everything else like that. She'd be driving and we'd have to follow her and uh because they wanted to make sure she got out of the area and wasn't working the boulevard."

Breitenstein: "How would you classify, uh Officer Avrech' s relationship with this individual?"

Tompkins: "Uh, relationship? There's no relationship. Every time I've been with him, he talks to her, you know, just like he talks to any, any other prostitute on the boulevard, you know, asks her the questions and uh, you know."

Moratto: "Okay, we talked about being truthful and totally honest during the investigation. There is no room for covering up for anybody, okay? And we explained to you this is, it's an administrative action, it's not a criminal action."

Moratto: "Now he's not asking you questions just out of the blue; he's asking you questions because he has some independent knowledge about the situation (Gentile). So, if you lie about any part of it, then your credibility is going with that."

Tompkins: "Uh-huh..."

But they didn't like the truth, they wanted to hear dirt. When they had no corroboration of what they wanted to hear, they had to re-admonish Steve to "tell the truth."

The subject regarding Officer Gulyas came up as to whether I asked Gentile to file a false complaint against him because we didn't get along. Tompkins denied any knowledge of that but said he knew I didn't get along with him.

Tompkins: "Yeah, they were, he worked at the Olympics. I wasn't there, so uh apparently, he (Gulyas) was in charge, not the Sergeant or anything but supposedly in charge of a group that rotated to different places (during the security watch) and all the officers didn't agree with the way he rotated, made the rotations, that Gulyas made the rotations, everybody complained about it."

The real reason he got on my bad side was prior to the Olympic security detail, I was assigned to work the Padre/Dodgers baseball game.

While at Jack Murphy Stadium, I broke up several fan fights and was involved in an after-game arrest in the stands of several people fighting with me. During the arrest, I received several blood stains on my uniform. I needed to go to the station just up the hill to change uniforms prior to going to my Olympic assignment.

When I arrived late, before I could explain the circumstances to Gulyas he says, "Where the fuck have you been? You're late!" This was the real cause of tension between us. I called from the station and notified an officer I'd be late. Obviously, the message never got to Gulyas.

The questioning of Tompkins continued.

Breitenstein: "Steve, uh we've been conducting a rather in-depth investigation regarding the things that we've, uh just discussed and I've gotta be real honest with you. I don't think you're telling me everything totally truthfully. I have some, uh, information that leads me to believe that some of these activities actually have taken place while you've been present with Officer Avrech."

Tompkins: "Uh, what activities is that?"

Breitenstein: "I think that there's more that's been taking place at this apartment complex than uh where this female, Donna Gentile lives and I think you've spent more time at that residence than you've told me. I'd like the truth. I'd like the truth about what's taken place out there at that apartment complex."

Tompkins: "That's it."

Breitenstein: "Has Officer Avrech ever had sexual intercourse while you were waiting in the car?"

Tomkins: "No."

To borrow a Jack Nicholson line from the movie "A Few Good Men." "They just couldn't handle the truth."

Breitenstein: "Five minutes is the longest he ever stayed up there?"

Tompkins: "Yeah."

Breitenstein: "Have you ever been inside her apartment?"

Tompkins: "No, he's never been either."

Moratto gave Tompkins a direct order not to discuss this interview with me. Yet, this interview and the way he was treated left a bad taste in his mouth about the department. Plus, the next time we saw each other, out of loyalty to me, he came out and told me what they said.

They concluded their interview by saying they appreciated his free time as a Reserve Officer and if they found out he discussed this matter with me he'd be subject to discipline.

Tompkins: "Yeah well, as long as you don't make it sound like a threat! You know I don't like to be threatened."

Moratto: "It's not a threat."

Breitenstein: "It's not a threat."

Tompkins: "Like I said, I'm out here (working) for nothing."

Moratto: "Okay, we realize that."

Tompkins: "So... I'm getting tired of it, too."

Moratto: "We know your position and we appreciate Reserve Officers out here; we know you guys."

Tompkins: "Yeah, I'll bet."

Moratto: "We're doing an investigation and we're not about to have our investigation fouled up by a Reserve. So, we do appreciate that, and we understand your uh bag. It's not and don't construe it as a threat."

Tompkins: "Well I do and I'll see my lawyer."

I never asked Steve whether he followed up and consulted an attorney.

MY UNFOUNDED HIT AND RUN

On September 26, 1984, I drove to Eastern Division for squad lineup. After lineup I grabbed my patrol car and pulled it over to where I parked my personal vehicle. Rather than carrying all my gear in my locker at work, I brought it home with me every night. As I opened the trunk to my 1980 Ford Mustang to transfer my gear to my squad car, I noticed a dent on the passenger side front quarter panel. My vehicle was parked inside the security fence at the Eastern Sub-Station. I noticed there was an impression made by another car brand on the panel. It was clearly the name of a Honda Civic showing the word Civic spelled backward.

The parking space next to me was vacant. Either someone hit my car and drove off or hit it and re-parked somewhere else. I parked my car in the driveway of my house and didn't leave home all day. Next to my car in the driveway was my other vehicle a yellow 1977 Datsun F-10.

I arrived just before 10:00 pm and walked out to find the damage at 10:40pm. So, it had to occur between when I arrived and the time of discovery. I went back inside and reported it. Instead of a traffic unit taking the report, Sergeant Barbara Harrison a traffic supervisor, took it instead. Traffic Sergeants don't take reports, they approve them from their officers. This was extremely unusual, plus a determination was made the accident didn't occur where I said it did. Also, it was an officer's report only and not given a case number.*

I didn't imagine it. It happened. No one parked next to me all day because I didn't leave the house all day. It was parked in my driveway next to my 1977 Datsun F-10. It wasn't damaged until after I came to work at night. This was the second of many dirty tricks pulled while I was under investigation.

ED DILLON, MY FIRST ATTORNEY THEN CARL BLACK'S ATTORNEY

On September 26, 1984, my Internal Affairs investigation was completed and sent back to my command with allegations from Gentile not sustained. There were also allegations that were sustained explained in Chapter 7.

My Captain was Tom Hall and he wanted to deepen the investigation and asked one of his patrol Lieutenant's William Skinner to reinvestigate the complaint. At the time I was working for a newly promoted Sergeant, Reggie Frank. Hall felt Skinner had more experience into these matters. Had Frank done my investigation he would've been completely impartial and cleared me of all allegations. Years later Reggie became the department Rangemaster. He told me, "Hey man, as far as I'm concerned, you're still on the department and I'll give you 100 rounds to shoot everyday if you want."

After being called in from the field one night and interrogated by Skinner, I stopped the procedure and sought counsel. I asked my association what attorneys were available. I needed the best. Word had circulated in the department James Gattey and Greg Petersen were the best; however, I was told neither were available. I was assigned Ed Dillon who specialized in Workman's Compensation cases. Not my idea of the best. This was like a foot doctor performing brain surgery.

After opening up and giving him all the information I collected against Carl Black, Dillon looked at me and said, "Listen, here's what's going to happen. You're gonna cop to all the allegations, you'll get a healthy suspension, but at least you'll keep your job."

I started to do a slow burn and said, "You're supposed to represent me to the best of your ability and in my best interests. I'm not going to admit to something I didn't do." I fired him on the spot and obtained Donald S. Peterson who represented me properly.

In June of 1985, Carl Black's Civil Service hearing was scheduled, and his attorney was Ed Dillon. Dillon should have declined to represent Black as he was my attorney in the same investigation. At the least it was a conflict of interests, but according to California Code of Professional Responsibility for attorneys, Dillon wasn't allowed to represent Black because he represented an adversarial position to mine without my written permission. I told the truth and spilled my guts to Dillon. Who knew what attorney/ client discussions with Dillon were passed onto Black to form a defense against any of my allegations. If I knew this was going on, I would have filed a motion and a judge would have disqualified Dillon.

THREATS AND INTIMIDATION OF OFFICERS BY LT. CONNIE VAN PUTTEN

While working the front counter since October of 1984, I was out of touch with my friends at Eastern Division. I was transferred to the old Central Division Headquarters at 801 W. Market Street. So, one day I called a few of my friends at Eastern to see what was going on and I received the following responses.

"Hey, I don't care, I don't want to know, I can't talk to you, I have a family to think about. Please don't call me, I have two more years to go, I just want to get my wristwatch, my lunch with the Chief and get out clean. I don't want to know, I'm sorry."

The absolute alienation was both overwhelming and devastating. These were people I raced to save when they called for cover. I broke bread with them. What was happening? I couldn't comprehend what I was hearing. Suddenly I became "Typhoid Mary" to my friends.

Then I received a call from a person I promised would remain nameless. I was told Lieutenant Connie Van Putten, a patrol Lieutenant at Eastern walked into police squad lineups and told the squads, "Larry Avrech is suffering from emotions, don't listen to him, don't talk to him, don't help him, if you do you may wind up in front of an appeals board."

Now it all made sense. They were being threatened with their jobs and intimidated if they so much as associated with me. How dare she threaten my friends and assassinate my character. If this wasn't the dirtiest trick of all dirty tricks, This was character assassination at its worst.

MY FIVE-YEAR PIN CEREMONY

My date of hire was November 8, 1979. After five years of service with the department, they award a City of San Diego five-year pin. It is worn on the uniform, along with a gold nameplate with a star for every five years of service. *

On or about the first week of November 1984, I failed to receive my pin and nameplate as was customary. I inquired about it to my command, but was told they'd look into it. In the past, other members received their pin and nameplate almost to the anniversary date as this is ordered in advance of the upcoming anniversary.

After being pulled out of the field, I was now assigned to the front counter at Central Headquarters. The front counter assignment included answering phones, verifying impounds, (money etc.) after hours, taking reports from citizens who walked in off the street to report crimes, buzzing people into the station after hours, providing directions to people and any other work the Duty Lieutenant or his aide gave me to do.

It is the duty Lieutenant's job to run the city, make decisions at incident scenes, approve bookings and contact homicide, gang or other investigative units to roll on an incident and notify Chief officers in the event of an Officer shooting or death. Duty Lieutenants were assigned normal five-day work weeks. Unless they're on a day off or on vacation, they remain the same person during their watch.

My hours were 11:00 pm -7:00 am. Sometimes it was busy from the time I got to work until quitting time. At other times it was quiet and boring. As a distraction, I'd bring the daily crossword puzzle with me to keep my wits sharp. It was also therapeutic to keep my mind off my impending doom.

Nancy Goodrich wasn't one of my favorite duty Lieutenants. She knew I was looking at termination and she was icily cold toward me. I respected her rank, but not her as a person. I couldn't and wouldn't be rude or disrespectful to her. So, this is how I dealt with her coldness.

She would ask me if I completed the crossword puzzle I brought in because she was having difficulty finishing it.

I told her "Yes, I did."

Then she'd ask if I got the answer to 45 across.

I'd reply, "Of course didn't you?"

Other nights, Mike Gillespie was the duty Lieutenant and I steered clear of him altogether. If looks could kill, need I say more. I was supposed to attend Advanced Officer's training at Camp Elliott. Even though his office was directly behind me where you could walk around the corner to his and rather than calling me back to his desk and talking to me, he wrote a memo and gave it to his aide to give me.*

The memo read, I was overlooked for training and I'd have to take it sometime next year. Of course he knew I would no longer be on the department, so it was easy for him to say. The next day I went to the training Lieutenant and was added to the class. Imagine, they had room for one more person.

These documents were used at my Civil Service hearing to show after I filed a grievance on behalf of my academy class for failing to give us our guaranteed step raises and won my case. My name was mud. The Chief who approved our grievance was Ken O'Brien, the same Chief who heard my appeal and recommended my termination. So, he let me win the battle because in the end he would win the war.

The duty Lieutenant I last worked for was Richard (Dick) Boas. One night on January 7, 1985, Dick called me back to his office. I walked around the corner to see what he wanted. His aide was also there in the office and Dick told him to close the door and stay. After the door was shut Dick said, "Larry I have seen these in my desk, (which he shared with the other duty Lieutenant's) for a while now and I think regardless of your current situation, I want to present you with your five-year city pin and your nameplate with your first five-year star. I think you've more than earned it and I want you to have it. Obviously, others didn't. I don't think you ever expected to receive it, but I wanted to make sure you did. He pinned it on my uniform and shook my hand and congratulated me.

His little gesture meant so much. I had told the truth and thought I'd done the right thing. I was proud to be a San Diego Police Officer. I received my pin and nameplate 15 days before my termination.

Dick then pulled out a sheet of paper from the desk. It was a complaint generated by Goodrich's aide reporting I'd asked for overtime to finish reports on a busy night. Dick handed me the complaint so I could read it.

He said, "You know what I'm going to do with this?" He took the complaint from me tore it up and gave it back to me saying, "That's what I think about you and Goodrich's aide." *

I was able to contact Dick after he retired and reminisce a little with him. Dick passed away December 22, 2016. You were a good friend and I salute you.

CHAPTER NINE

ODDITIES -YOU DECIDE

I won the battle but was losing the war. I previously mentioned in Chapter 2 when I first had a target on my back. From the time I first filed a grievance over my academy class pay issue. This was long before the Gentile investigation.

I was passed over for field training officer, "Nora" unit training which consisted of officers who were specially trained to handle crime scenes. They carried a box full of supplies for gathering evidence and special powders for lifting difficult fingerprints, etc. Detectives from various investigative bureaus requested I receive investigative training with their unit. I was asked by Sergeant Dave Elliott from Robbery division to work their "Star" detail. This was a special enforcement detail they ran between Thanksgiving and the first of the year. Undercover patrol and robbery units were added to the field during the holidays when liquor stores, grocery stores, banks and large businesses dealt with larger cash amounts and were prime targets for robberies. Sergeant Jake Jacobson from Fencing also requested I work two weeks with their unit. Detective Steve Baker from Special investigations also requested I work with their unit.

Even from my own division at Eastern, Gerry Tacoronte, an Eastern Division detective requested I spend two weeks with him for investigative training. The answers were all the same. Sorry, manpower shortages, can't spare you, maybe next time. Even if I received the okay from the units themselves, I could never get it passed from my command. The street survival seminar I went to in Morton Grove, Illinois I wound up using my vacation time and paying for it out of my own pocket. The FBI special antiterrorism training I attended for the upcoming Olympics in 1984 was only because I talked to my friend and SWAT commander John Morrison who found another seat for me.

During the time I was on the department and after my termination, I was subjected to various incidents. I will describe these and let you decide if they were merely coincidences or done with malice. Additionally, I researched information on my case and the players involved and will let you decide.

On May 12, 1983 officers Avrech, Jaus, McDermed, Prutzman and Candland responded to a rape in progress. Working in concert, these officers contacted the victim, witnesses and stopped several possible suspects. Officer Jaus recalled a suspect in a series of indecent exposure cases who lived in the immediate area who matched the description of the assault suspect. He set up a stake out on the subject's house. He returned ninety minutes later and was taken into custody. The victim positively identified the suspect during a curbstone line up. All officers involved received a commendation for their teamwork and coordinated efforts. The procedure for receiving a commendation is to have the command sign it, give a separate copy to the officer or officers involved and read it at lineup. I never received the commendation and a copy of it with a note written in a woman's handwriting stating,* "Put in Larry's jacket, he never rec'd it. Wasn't even aware of it. They never read it at lineup for Larry like it should have been. They did read it for everyone else though. All officers are supposed to sign a commendation they receive." You decide.

On August 11, 1984 Donna Gentile went to Sergeant Harold Goudarzi, my Eastern Division Sergeant at the time with allegations of misconduct against me. They drove to the Denny's restaurant in the College Grove area and he took a recorded interview from her.

The interview ran into the early hours of August 12. Goudarzi wrote up a supervisor's investigation report.

The following day a supervisor's report was submitted to my investigative Lieutenant Ron Seden. He turned the report over to Internal Affairs detectives on August 14, 1984 and Gentile was again interviewed at a non-disclosed location in the City of Lemon Grove by Internal Affairs Lieutenant Les Ginn and Sergeants Glenn Breitenstein and Harold Goudarzi. There is only a mention of this meeting. There's no taped interview or written interview only a statement by Breitenstein. Gentile essentially said the same things as she previously stated. Why was there no interview? Did Gentile mention to them her association with Carl Black? I don't think so. He was her sugar daddy. It would be her reason for turning me in, to keep the money coming from him.

When they interviewed my reserve partner on August 21, 1984, he told investigators he heard a rumor about Carl Black taking Donna and some Sergeants and their family members to the Colorado River for a weekend.*

I was interviewed for the first time on August 22, 1984.* However, Breintenstein's report reflects he interviewed me on August 16, 1984 according to the documents he read and signed. This is impossible, because I was first interviewed when Internal Affairs tape recorded our telephone conversations between August 15th and August 21st 1984. Once again, the three interviewed her, but there was no recorded interview, just Breitenstein's word in his report. The two interviews with Gentile were essentially the same. Why were there no recorded interview or notes taken during the meeting?

In the Internal Affairs investigative packet there are reports of tape-recorded telephone conversations between Gentile and me. There was a total of nine recorded conversations starting August 15, 1984 through August 21, 1984, into the early morning.*

Later the same day, my reserve partner was called in and interviewed in the afternoon. I wasn't called in until August 22, 1984 and again on August 27, 1984. Yet Breitenstein's report indicates I was called in on August 16,1984.* There was no interview conducted with me on August 16, 1984. Two possible theories exist: First, they asked her to cooperate with them in their investigation of me and first set up tape-recording equipment on her apartment phone. The first of two tape recorded conversations took place August 15, 1984. The typed transcript heading indicated it was for the exclusive use of the Chief of Police and/or the City Attorney. The next transcribed taped conversation heading, recorded August 17, 1984 indicates, "During the course of a criminal investigation, involving officer Larry Avrech, a "cooperating individual," Donna Marie Gentile, (notice she wasn't deemed a police informant or a prostitute under criminal investigation) was directed by Sergeant Glenn Breitenstein to tape record any telephone conversation between herself and the subject officer. So, from August 11 -August 16, 1984 this was an administrative investigation. However, on August 17, 1984 it became a criminal investigation. There are no other headings for the remaining six taped conversations where they indicated it became a criminal investigation until August 21, 1984, when they interviewed my reserve partner and told him it was an administrative investigation.

The following day when I was brought into Internal Affairs for the first time, I was instructed by Sergeant Breitenstein this was an administrative investigation.* So, which is it a criminal investigation or an administrative investigation?

My second theory is Internal Affairs made it a criminal investigation to skirt around the penal code which states to intercept calls, it is necessary to require a court order or have a violent felony occurring to get around the law. There was no court order or violent felony.

You decide.

Between August 22-23 Internal Affairs finished recording our conversations. Gentile's car was broken into the night she returned to the boulevard. I wonder whether they ever admonished her to stop committing crimes if she ever wanted to work for the department again. I obtained a copy of the case *Gentile phoned into the telephone report unit. Unusual, just a coincidence?

You decide.

Gentile filed a harassment suit against seven members of the department but was killed before she could take it to court. What she considered harassment was a form of selective enforcement to drive women off the El Cajon Boulevard corridor, hoping they'd move to other areas of the city or leave town completely. Of the seven officers named in the complaint my name wasn't in the mix.

Another oddity was when Gentile opened the door to her apartment you could visibly see a San Diego County Sheriff's Department decal generally secured to a Sheriffs squad car door, affixed to the wall behind her. She lived at the Spring Hill Apartments in La Mesa, California at 4341 Spring Street #47. The property management company handling the property was, Cono (Charles Cono), Hanken (Gene Hanken) and Assad (Alfred Assad Jr. aka Spring Hill Associates located at 6526 El Cajon Boulevard, the area Gentile worked. Charles Cono was also a San Diego County Honorary Deputy Sheriff.

Gentile was served with an unlawful detainer at the woman's jail, Las Colinas for non-payment of rent on March 18, 1985 by Attorney Michael Barnes. He handled the legal evictions for Cono and Hanken. Obviously, they knew she was in jail rather than at work or out of town. Additionally, Cono with his association with the Sheriff's department, could've made a phone call and found out she was in jail.

The San Diego County Sheriff at the time was John Duffy. While in office he made the mistake of sending out cards indicating Rose Bird, Chief Justice for the California Supreme court should step down from her position. Duffy was investigated and fined $36,000. Three people stepped up and paid his fine. They were Arthur Bloom, owner of the now defunct Worth's on the Boulevard department store located at 3033 El Cajon Boulevard. Charles Cono of Cono and Hanken and William Cowling owner of Dixieline Lumber and a Captain with the San Diego County Honorary Deputy Sheriff's department. All three were members of the Nice Guys club as well as Chief Bill Kolender. Arthur Bloom, prior to purchasing the property lived in a home in La Jolla, California owned by former Attorney James Pasto, Bar # 48445. He was known at the courthouse as "the Hooker Attorney." Pasto was disbarred in 2014 for professional misconduct. The address was 5904 Camino De La Costa, which is currently owned by the Barbara and Arthur Bloom family trust. Merely a coincidence? You decide.

Another oddity was the fact that Captain Mike Tyler, head of the Criminal Intelligence unit of the San Diego Police department dealt with prostitute Cynthia Maine added to the list of murdered prostitutes. Tyler also owned Tyler's feed in Alpine which supplied hay and grain to the stable where Donna Gentile rode her horse, Fantasia.

Before retiring Tyler was the Captain at Eastern Division who ordered Sergeant Joe Cunningham and his officers not to cooperate with the Sheriff's Department personnel investigating the Gentile homicide. When Tyler testified before the Grand Jury in 1989-1990 the Jury Foreman, J. Phil Franklin in the Grand Jury's report felt Chief Kolender and Mike Tyler were less than truthful experiencing frequent memory lapses. The Jury wanted to indict them on perjury charges but were advised against it by Chief Deputy District Attorney Brian Michaels.

In April of 1985, I could no longer afford the rent for my comic book business, so I moved the bookshelves and store contents into the living room of my house. I hooked up my business phone and attached an answering machine with a pre-recorded message. I left a message letting customers know what books were coming in weekly and they would leave a message with their order. During this time, I received a lot of hang-up calls. This worked well and I continued making money from book sales.

Suddenly, my phone stopped working on June 14, 1985. I called the phone company who came out and said I had to disconnect the answering machine for my phone to work again. I was also charged for their visit.* June 14,1985 was the same date my old Sergeant Harold Goudarzi was transferred to Internal Affairs from Eastern Division. I was later told by the phone company, when a phone is tapped it puts an extra load on the line. The technician told me after he disconnected the answering machine my phone would work again. After he left, I reconnected my answering machine with no further problems. This is how I figured the department knew my wife contacted 60 Minutes. It was only mentioned on the phone and in another chapter where my ex-wife was contacted by Sergeant Breitenstein. * She asked him, if he tapped my phone. There was a long pause with no answer. Other intelligence officers indicated to me this is done often. Was it a coincidence or a malicious act?

You decide.

Also, in June of 1985, I came home after work and noticed the outside light was out. As I approached my front door, I discovered my double cylinder deadbolt lock was removed from my security screen door and in two pieces on the ground. I opened the inner door and walked inside to check out my house. I turned the light switch on, and nothing happened. I got a flashlight, walked outside to the box and found the lock snipped and on the ground. My main power switch was turned off. A thorough search of my house indicated nothing seemed to be disturbed or stolen. Why remove my lock and turn my power off? Coincidence or malicious intent?

You decide.

June of 1985 was a rough month for me all around. I started receiving phone calls from creditors asking why I didn't send in payments on time. I told them I wasn't billed and advised them to send my monthly bills to me. Apparently my mail was being interrupted or removed from my mailbox when I was away. The only people I could think who had knowledge of what bills I owed was the Police Department. I tried to get a hardship loan from my association in October of 1984 when I was still a member. I spoke to Detective Vince Krolikowski who handled the Hardship Committee for the Police Officer's Association. I went in and discussed my case and he asked me what I needed to cover my bills. I gave him a list of my bills at the time. When Vince left the room to get coffee, I turned over the manila folder with my name on it. A note read, "Do not help Avrech he has gone to the F.B.I." Initially I thought the department would help me by seeing how much money I needed to cover my bills. All they truly wanted was to know how badly I was hurting. Was this another coincidence or a malicious act?

You decide.

In October of 1984, I was still working Eastern Division graveyard shift from 11:00 pm to 7:00 am. It was an 18-mile drive home for me. The minute I got home I'd change out of my uniform and went to bed. Not more than 20 minutes after going to bed, the phone rang. It was Sergeant Breitenstein from Internal Affairs telling to come downtown and meet with him.

I told him I just worked the night shift and if he wanted to talk to me, he could see me at work. My wife took the phone from me and told him they were violating my civil rights and she was calling the FBI.

The same night I got ready for work, got in my car and started the ignition. There was a loud explosion from under the hood. It scared the hell out of me, and I rolled out onto the driveway. My wife came out screaming and thought I was dead. We called the Sheriff's Department. Conrad Grayson from the Bomb Squad came out. He talked on the phone with the duty Lieutenant as I was in no shape to drive or go to work.

My Sergeant was now Bob Stinson. He was asked to respond to see if I was telling the truth about not coming in. Grayson spoke on the phone and after a few minutes told me the explosion wasn't deliberate. There's no way to make a battery explode. It had to be hydrogen gas escaping from the battery and a spark ignited it. He didn't spend much time looking under my hood to make a snap decision about the origin of the explosion.

In fact,, you can make a car battery explode using a turkey baster. If the battery acid is removed and the lead plates inside are exposed to oxygen, they can build up an explosive charge which can be triggered by a spark from the ignition. Was this a coincidence or a malicious act?

You decide.

A week or two later I was trimming the bushes between my property and my neighbor to the north of me at about 9:00 am in the morning. I noticed a glass container with something burning in it. I picked it up and it burned my hands. I quickly put it out. There was a flammable substance with a petroleum odor, like jelly gasoline or what's often used to light barbecues called Fire Wax. It was in a small glass jar. There was writing on the inside of the jar and all I could make out was the word "photo." After having a report taken, I never heard anything about it until January when my attorney requested my

Deputy, Chief Ken O'Brien look into it. After O'Brien told Bill Skinner the Lieutenant from Eastern Division who reinvestigated my case to look into it, he contacted the Sheriff's Department and was told the substance couldn't be identified. Was it done to scare me? What do you think? A coincidence or a malicious act?

You decide.

On October 20, 1984 I received a notice of violation from the City of Santee.* It read an inspection was done of my property by the Santee Planning Department. They found the chicken coop in my backyard wasn't according to code and I was given two weeks to correct the problem or go to court. Until I received this notice, I had chickens for four years with no problem. It didn't seem right at the same time as when everything else was happening.

I tore down the coop and got rid of the chickens. I wasn't going to appear before a Judge and be fined. I don't think it was a coincidence. I think someone called the City who knew about the chicken coop. There was an open field behind our house and I got along well with my neighbors on both sides. This may be a coincidence or maybe not.

You decide.

On November 12, 1985 I received a notice to vacate my house from the San Diego County Marshal's office. I was given six days from November 18, 1985 to move out.* I was out at the prescribed time and drove to my storage unit to store the contents of my house. I spent the night at the house of my Postal Inspector friend Thomas Hofius. He lived in San Carlos at 7654 Jennite Drive just over the hill from Santee. At 1:15 am in the morning we were all awakened by the sound of the Sheriff's Department A.S.T.R.E.A. helicopter. Their searchlight was shining directly in Tom's backyard. It was a well-known fact A.S.T.R.E.A. went to bed so to speak at its airport hangar at Gillespie Field at midnight, unless they were on call for service in our area or another jurisdiction. A check the next day indicated no prowlers, missing children or suspects on the loose, especially in my friend's backyard. No authorization was given for them to be in the area. Was this a coincidence or another malicious act?

You decide.

I was going out of town the next morning. I was offered an opportunity to drive a truck with a trailer carrying a race car to the Phoenix airport, meet the owner collect $100.00 and a plane ticket back to San Diego. About 60 miles outside San Diego off Interstate 8 freeway the steering on the truck went out and the trailer fishtailed behind me, leaving the road. I was forced off the road, down an embankment and rolled over three times.*I dove out the window, crawled up to the freeway and was transported by ambulance to Grossmont Hospital with only bumps and bruises.* The California Highway Patrol Officer told me he moved the steering wheel and the tires moved so there was nothing wrong with the truck. Unfortunately, when dealing with a rollover accident, I'd prefer someone in a white lab coat to tell me. Did someone tamper with the truck's steering? Absolutely. But I leave it up to you. Was this a coincidence or a malicious act?

You decide.

CHAPTER TEN

MESSING WITH MY FAMILY

DURING MY LIFETIME I've worked many jobs and observed many people who were terminated. I've been fired myself, but once a person was gone, they were never more than an afterthought. The terminated person was replaced and life went on, unless they were a San Diego Police officer. Cross them and you remain in their crosshairs forever. They would launch a personal campaign to ultimately destroy the person who was terminated.

I was officially terminated on January 22,1985. Over two weeks afterward it was evident my ex-wife was being followed. Her current husband was out to sea.

On Wednesday night February 6, 1985, upon returning home from bowling night, my ex-wife Susan noticed a police business card wedged in her door. It was from Sergeant Glenn Breitenstein, from Internal Affairs. The message on the card requested she call him between 8:00am and 4:00pm.

Susan recognized the name and knew her mother worked for his wife

Bonnie at a bank. Susan called her mother to ask if she was contacted as well.

She replied, "No."

Susan called Breitenstein the following day from work. He asked her if she was married to an officer, Larry Avrech?

She replied, "Yes."

He asked if she knew I was no longer on the force or suspended?

She answered, "Yes."

He asked her when she last saw me?

She responded, "Tuesday night." She saw me every day because I had custody of our children.

Breitenstein stated the reason for his call because I mentioned his wife Bonnie and my mother in-law worked together. He changed the facts purposefully, accusing Susan's mother (not Susan) of being involved in an embezzlement case.

The truth was my ex-wife, Susan was a treasurer for the A.B.W.A. American Business Women's Association and used the group's funds for her own purposes. I gave a speech at one of their meetings on home security and after an audit it was discovered funds were missing. I was still on probation with the department and could've lost my career just by guilt by association.

I was contacted by the president of the group who planned on reporting it to the Sheriff's Department if the money wasn't paid back in seven days. I went to my credit union and borrowed the money to repay them.

Breitenstein somehow knew this and I asked him to take himself off the investigation and put someone else on it due to a conflict of interest. I didn't know whether he discussed department business with his wife and Susan didn't want her mother involved.

Breitenstein was aware of the true facts, but by twisting the facts, he made it appear as if my mother in-law was embezzling from the bank. He tried to get Susan angry at me to the point where she'd help the department by testifying against me at my Civil Service Hearing.

It didn't work. Susan called me, and we discussed it. She also wrote me a six-page letter which outlined their phone conversation verbatim.*

Susan was asked to tell Breitenstein about the embezzlement case. She felt compelled to tell him by his tone of voice even though he said she didn't have to tell him. Susan mentioned she was glad she was in a private office. She told Breitenstein she took the funds and they were repaid. She also said she resented the fact her mother was implicated.

Breitenstein asked Susan about my mental condition when we were married and any observations she noticed.

Susan told him, "No offense, but I know very few cops with all their marbles in one bag."

Breitenstein replied, "No offense taken. That's my job, to weed out the bad ones."

Susan told Breitenstein I was under pressure for what was happening at the department. I had gathered a lot more evidence and would release it to the press if necessary.

Breitenstein asked Susan, "Who could pressure me?"

Susan replied, "Work" and I tended to bend to pressure from women.

Breitenstein said, "I gathered that. Do you know of anything specific?"

Susan said most of what she knew was conjecture from conversations with him and his current wife, Paula. Also, from a letter I typed for them.

Breitenstein inquired as to who the letter was addressed to and what it said? *

Susan told him it was addressed to the TV show 60 Minutes. There was nothing definite in the letter only that Paula's husband would be fired from the San Diego Police Department unjustly and asked for their help in exposing the cover-up. Susan further stated a Lieutenant was involved. No names or dates were mentioned.

Breitenstein asked, "Did you write the letter?"

Susan said, "No."

He asked, "Did Larry write the letter?"

Susan said, "No."

Breitenstein wanted to know, "Do you have any copies or carbons of the letter?

Susan said, "I don't think so, but I'll check."

Breitenstein asked, "Are there other people involved?"

Susan said, "I don't know any names, but I know he's not acting alone.

Breitenstein asked, "Will you testify against Larry at the Civil Service hearing?"

She was quiet for a minute and then asked, "Will Larry be there?"

Breitenstein said, "Yes."

Susan was quiet again and said softly, "If it's absolutely necessary, I will. However, if I found out my testimony stops an investigation into major problems in the department, there would be a whole new set of problems." Susan had no idea if I was guilty or innocent, but she knew I didn't make wild accusations.

Breitenstein asked, "Did Larry ever lie to you?"

Susan snapped back, "Have you ever lied to your wife?"

Breitenstein said, "That's not the question."

Susan replied, "I'm sure he has."

Breitenstein asked Susan about when she had the kids.

Susan asked, "Is it true the Police has tapped Larry's phones?"

Breitenstein never answered.

Susan told him when she had the kids.

Breitenstein asked Susan, "When do you think Larry meets with 'those other people?'"

Susan stated, "Possibly Sundays," but it could've been at any time. She didn't care. Changing the subject, she asked, "Is it okay for Larry to wear a gun in the comic bookstore?"

Breitenstein replied, "Yes."

Susan told him she was concerned about the kids being in the store.

Breitenstein told her to go see an attorney.

Susan shared this in a phone call to me. Breitenstein also told her she needed to get the kids away from me because terrible things would be happening to me. The kids shouldn't be around to see.

Wait a minute what kind of terrible things would happen to me? How would he know? Wasn't I terminated already? What possible things would they drop in my lap to further harass me? It reminded me of a World War II fighter ace following his kill to the ground. It wasn't enough to shoot me up, then they had to follow their kill down to the ground.

Breitenstein asked if Susan, "Do you know if Larry's ever been under investigation before? (Gentile Ride A Long, refer to Chapter 3)

She stated, "I'm not sure if it really was an investigation." You may recall all the questioning I got after the ride-along with Gentile back in Chapter 3.

A cop came to the house saying he was investigating Larry regarding a concern about a prostitute. She never heard any more about it.

Breitenstein asked her, "Does Larry make a habit of investigating others?"

Susan said, "If Larry thinks there's a good reason, yes. Ray Hoobler, ex-Chief of Police and head of security for the Atlas Hotels did that very thing."

The reason I was let go from Atlas was because there was an internal investigation ongoing with members of the criminal intelligence unit of the police department. Employee files were stolen in an effort to make a list of people to contact and organize a union. I was a corporate security officer and was talking with a phone dispatcher at the hotel who was involved with the Food and Beverage Manager. She was shooting off her mouth to me.

I just nodded and smiled as she talked to me. I was receiving information faster than the undercover operatives were and Hoobler felt it might comprimise their case, When I lost my job with the Atlas Hotels I really didn't understand it at the time, but I was able to understand it years later. I've continued to have contact with Ray over the years on a friendly basis.

Breitenstein told Susan, "I'm trying to ascertain Larry's mental stability. Are you afraid of him?"

Susan said, "No, but I was deeply hurt by the divorce."

Breitenstein told Susan not to reveal this conversation to me. His voice and demeanor were ominous, intimidating and scared her a little. A second time he mentioned he was checking my mental stability.

Breitenstein again asked her to search for the letter to 60 Minutes and call him. He added he realized Susan was very upset and once again warned her not to discuss it with me.

The impression Susan got from Breitenstein was she was in some sort of danger from me.

The next morning Susan thought she was followed to work and home as well as when she went to pick up the kids.

The next week, Breitenstein called her at work asking again about the 60 Minutes letter.

Susan told him she couldn't find any copies or carbons.

Breitenstein hoped she would have found it.

Also, in the phone conversation of February 7, 1985 when Susan said she wouldn't want her testimony to interfere with a proper investigation, Breitenstein stated, Lieutenant Black had been under investigation for a long time. Steps were being taken for his hearing soon. However, he said Larry hindered rather than helped the investigation into Black.

First, Carl Black was a Lieutenant in Communications in 1981* along with Sergeant Breitenstein, and Sergeant Connie Van Putten. They all worked together so bringing information about Black to Breitenstein would have prevented a proper investigation. He was also aware of a sexual harassment investigation surrounding Black with one of the dispatchers while he was there. Van Putten later became my Lieutenant at Eastern. Oh, what a tangled web we weave.

CHAPTER ELEVEN

CIVIL SERVICE HEARING

SOMETHING WASN'T RIGHT. Why did they believe a prostitute over me? My career was in jeopardy. Everything I worked so hard for was down the drain based on the lies of a prostitute. Something was going on and I had to get to the bottom of it. Local news stations jump-started their programs with my picture for everyone to see in San Diego. The unsustained allegations were out there for all of San Diego to hear and salivate over.

My Attorney at the time was Donald S. Peterson. He immediately filed a request for a hearing with the city and was waiting for acceptable dates to be given. Looking at the situation from all angles; for starters I was sweating it out doing the hurry up and wait game. Time and the unknown were my worst enemies.

I heard from Richard Boas a Lieutenant friend, he overheard a conversation where it was said, "If we don't fire Black, Avrech's got a case." Carl was initially given a ten-day suspension and transferred but was later terminated for contacting a probation officer regarding Gentile.

Black requested a hearing with Police Chief Bill Kolender. He reinstated Black, but reduced his rank to Sergeant for a year.

My ex-wife typed a letter to Mike Wallace of 60 Minutes and somehow, they learned about it. They grilled her about the contents of the letter. Why should they worry, unless they were hiding something? But they were.

Lowell Bergman, a producer at 60 Minutes remarked, "Sounds like they're up to their old tricks again. I guess we'll have to come out and see what this is all about."

60 Minutes investigated the Yellow Cab Scandal several years prior. They sent out Rich Bonin who is a leading producer with 60 Minutes today. Bonin came to the comic bookstore I owned. He spoke to former officers who were unjustly fired and gave me information on a local newspaperman I could trust. I took his advice months later.

My immediate concerns were for my family, our house, the children and our animals. I withdrew all my pension funds because I was two months behind on the mortgage and the $7,000. would catch me up and pay for food and bills. In addition, my income from the comic book store was my only income for a while going forward. I feared for my kids. Could I keep food in their mouths, clothes on their backs and a roof over their heads?

Was Civil Service a fair system or just a rubber stamp? I was sweating it out and not sleeping nights, lying awake wondering whether if I'd be reinstated as a San Diego Police Officer. I heard stories of other officers winning and being reinstated. One officer was fired for leaving contraband under the rear seat of his patrol car. When things weren't looking up for him, his friend took a trash bag, filled it with contraband left behind in numerous vehicles and noisily dumped the contents all over the table in front of the commission. He got his job back. Obviously, the truth alone wasn't enough in his case. It needed to be" jaw dropping" spectacular.

Donna Gentile was serving a six-month jail sentence for prostitution and was released the first week of May, 1985.

When interviewed by Internal Affairs detectives, Gentile was asked, "Did Larry Avrech threaten you?"

To which she replied," No"

Next, she was told, "But you felt threatened." They played it up to the hilt when she testified for the city against me. One of my squad partners Dorine Molinoski was her police guard. The Department even went so far as to buy her a dress and pearls, so she didn't look like a prostitute, but more like "Little Bo Peep." Additionally, she was provided with a deadbolt lock installed on her apartment door at city expense. Sergeant Goudarzi stood by at her apartment while it was installed. But after being evicted, she was now living at 4794 Utah street with Michelle Tennies a friend of hers, who rode horses together with Donna.

My hearing dates were set for May 7, May 8, May 15, May 16, June 4, June 19, July 2, and July 3. My Captain, Tom Hall from Eastern Division was called and upon cross examination he stated they discussed various strategies to entrap me. My attorney asked him to name one instance where they could trap me.

Hall said they considered trapping me over at Gentile's apartment. When asked if they did it Hall replied, "No, we decided against it." Truth be told, the reason why it wasn't used against me was because I couldn't be compromised. I was honest, with morals and integrity and would never do anything like sleeping with a prostitute to my wife. Even if I were single, I wouldn't choose to have sex with a prostitute.

When Goudarzi took the stand, he mentioned Donna couldn't be trusted. She was a problem they dealt with. After other girls left the Boulevard, she was "a diehard" and kept coming back. Things seemed to be looking up for me since the department's witnesses were making positive remarks in my favor.

On May 16, Gentile took the stand and either recanted her earlier allegations or she couldn't remember what she previously said. She testified for almost three hours and said I gave her confidential information regarding the location of officers making prostitution busts on El Cajon Boulevard. However, when questioned by my attorney, she could only provide details of one instance involving a vague description of my whereabouts. This is directly from a tape-recorded conversation by Gentile provided to Internal Affairs Sergeant Glenn Breitenstein. The conversation was:

Gentile: "Are you going to be out there?"

Avrech: "Yes."

Gentile: "Where will you be?"

Avrech: "I'll be at my end."

Gentile: "What is your end?"

Avrech: "The west end."

This was the substance of the questions and my answers. Now, everyone from San Diego would know and I'm sure most police officers knew regardless of their assignment and assigned area, no officer stays in one spot. Police officers rove, take reports or respond to calls for assistance. So in effect, I wasn't telling her anything about my whereabouts at all. But the department made an ambiguous statement fit their parameters. In addition, Eastern Patrol and Vice are lined up in different substations and they don't discuss their activities with us. They're a completely different entity and I'd have no information regarding how their detail was being carried out. My command knew this already.

My feelings were mixed. How would the three-person panel of Civil Service Commission take in the testimony? The panel included Commission President James McFarland, and Commissioners Dale

Cobb and Hope Logan. These people are citizens appointed by the Mayor with approval of the City Council. Hope Logan and Dale Cobb continued making eye contact with me throughout the hearing, regardless of who was speaking. They asked good questions and Hope Logan would occasionally smile at me. On a break in the men's room, not knowing I was there, I heard McFarland say he wanted this over quickly because he was going away on a cruise. I thought he was bored with the idea of sitting through the hearing and wasn't interested in listening. I felt his mind was made up before the hearing even started.

One of my witnesses was supposed to be George Varela, an officer working in the Chief's Office as his assistant. He drove out to my comic book store to talk with me. I thought if I had his ear I'd be back to work and could wake up from this nightmare. When George and I were together I asked him why they believed Donna Gentile over me?

He looked me in the eye and said, "Because it fits the specific needs of the department at this particular time."

I thought to myself wow, he is a friend willing to tell the truth and help me. Plus, he's a representative of the Chief's office. Even though I was under investigation, we both had to qualify at the pistol range later the same evening. I remembered his words to me. I asked him to repeat what he said. He repeated it word for word as if he was reading it from a script. "Because it fits the specific needs of the department at this particular time."

So, I planned to subpoena him to my Civil Service hearing. But when interviewed by my Investigator he lied claiming "I never said that." Yet he said it to me twice on the same day. Once in my comic book store, and once later in the evening at the Police Pistol Range. I thought his testimony would help me get back to work. So much for thinking.

As it turned out he only wanted to find out what I knew and was willing to tell him, so the department could stay one step ahead of me.

On June 4, I gave my testimony and refuted the allegations. On June 19, my wife gave testimony as to our parts in the investigation. She was aware of everything said and done from the date I stopped Gentile and Hughes, her ex-fiancé, going forward. My next hearing date was scheduled for July 2 and July 3, for closing arguments from both sides.

Since my termination, I bought three different newspapers almost every day. I read every article about what the department, the press and electronic media was reporting about me and the case. I collected, cut out and preserved every item. On Tuesday June 25, a three-inch article appeared in the morning edition of the San Diego Union. The headline said, "Woman's Body Found in Pine Valley" * A nude, unidentified white female mid 20's was found Sunday evening around 8:00 pm by a man exercising his dog. The article stated the body was discovered two miles north of Interstate 8 about 300 yards southwest of the Sunrise Highway A cold chill ran through my body. I hoped it wasn't Gentile. The article finished with the statement advising an autopsy was scheduled late the previous day.

On July 2, we asked the Civil Service Commission to dismiss the case for insufficient evidence, the motion was denied. Both sides were to give arguments. Walking out of the hearing my attorney told me the Commission's decision would normally take 40-45 days.

Upon returning home I checked the flashing light on my answering machine. There was a message from Channel 8 reporter friend Dave Cohen He was one of the reporters who listened to my story and even came out to my comic book store to talk with me. He also gave me fifty dollars, so I had money to feed my kids. His haunting message stated, "Larry, it's Dave Cohen from Channel 8 I hope you're not planning on suing Donna Gentile. They just found her body in Pine Valley."

A cold chill ran through me. I thought the small article I read eight days ago must have been her. My first thought was, oh my God, they killed her to frame me. I just became an instant suspect.

The police department wasn't commenting, but their silence was just as damning. I collected my thoughts putting my hands to my temples. I was visibly shaken. I sat there for a few minutes trying to compose myself. My heart felt like it would beat out of my chest.

After a few minutes I got up and tried calling my attorney, but I couldn't punch the number properly as my hands were still shaking. Finally, I reached him to tell him what I just learned.

"He said, Oh my goodness! I can't believe it," He instructed to stay in touch with him and not to speak with anyone.

People were putting two plus two together and coming up with the wrong conclusion. They were starting to suspect I killed her in retaliation. They assumed Officer Avrech associated with her, she turned him in, she testified against him, now she's dead. It was simple, easy and made sense. But that wasn't true and now I was fighting for my life.

The July 4, issue of The San Diego Union included a follow-up article.* It stated the nude body was found in the brush about 300 feet west of Sunrise Highway two miles north of Interstate 8. A blue shirt dress, a white cloth jacket and a pair of shoes were piled on the body.

The July 6, article from the San Diego Union indicated she was beaten and strangled. According to the Sheriff's Investigators their hunch was she was killed elsewhere, and her body dumped at the scene.

For a moment, let's examine Carl Black's Civil Service hearing. It was scheduled for June 25 and June 26. He wasn't fighting for his job like me. He was only fighting to restore his rank from Sergeant back to Lieutenant. Or, would he have to wait a year the department suggested for the disciplinary action meted against him?

First, we now know Gentile was already dead but still unidentified. The article about the body found was in the June 25 edition of the San Diego Union, which would have hit the streets early in the morning of June 25. The "Bulldog Edition" of the San Diego Union would've come out shortly after midnight on June 24.

The coroner said her body laid there where it was dumped at least a day before being found. An autopsy was scheduled for June 24. After taking pictures of the deceased, collecting evidence at the crime scene, the hands and feet of the victim are bagged. Once transported to the morgue, fingerprints are taken. The Coroner and members of the Sheriff's department and the San Diego Police Department were likely aware of her identity as early as June 24, yet the press wasn't informed until July 3, my last hearing day over a week later. Who knows if Gentile was even on the witness list by the department or by Black? Who knows what she would have said? We'll never know.

On July 10, (my birthday) I heard from the Civil Service Commission my termination was upheld. This wasn't the 30 or 45 days I was told I'd have to wait. My attorney suggested the Commission was aware of Gentile's death before making their decision. If this were a criminal case, it would've been grounds for a mistrial because the Commission didn't give a fair, unbiased verdict. Otherwise, why would they have made their decision in less than seven days? This was unprecedented.

I didn't feel the Commission listened to the evidence presented. Plus, I was tried by the press. My department let me down and the Commission followed suit. I have yet to be contacted by the Sheriff's Department.

In later issues of the newspaper the extent of Gentile's injuries were revealed. The media had a field day reporting this grisly discovery. The rocks and gravel in her mouth were thought to be a message she was killed because she was a snitch and spoke up.

CHAPTER TWELVE

DIRTY TRICKS II

I was working the front counter at the old San Diego Central Headquarters. Michelle Milam and I were having lunch. We had lunch together frequently while waiting to take officers to and from court. She drove the court shuttle van to transport officers from Central Headquarters to and from court.

Everything was laughs and giggles one day, when suddenly Lieutenant Ron Seden came in and called me away to an office across the hallway.

He instructed me to close the door and sit down. I stood over him while he sat behind a desk. He cleared his throat, clasped his hands together and with a steady gaze said, "Larry, it's the decision of the Chief you should be terminated." It was January 22, 1985.

What a crushing blow. My heart sank, but I couldn't let him see how much his words hurt inside. My career was over. Everything I worked so hard for was gone. Why was this happening? Why did they believe a prostitute over me? Nothing made sense.

Seden asked for my badge and police ID card.

I took my badge off my uniform and looked at it one more time. Badge #1677. I placed it on his desk with my ID card.

He said, "I'll need your gun."

I told him, "The gun is mine."

"But the bullets belong to the city," was his retort.

I drew my gun out of the "Judge Model" holster as quick as I could, which startled Seden for a moment. He pulled backward in his office chair. I turned the revolver to the side, emptied the bullets into my hand and placed them on the desk. I pointed to my badge, looked him straight in the eye and said, "I'll be back for my badge."

Seden said, "We'll hold onto it for you."

After handing over my squad car keys, shotgun key and signal box key, I was dismissed. It was a sucker punch to the gut, I was devastated. How could they do this? I swore I'd get to the bottom of everything and clear my good name.

I walked back across the hallway to get a few personal items I'd brought in from the front counter. Michelle was still there. She asked, "What's the matter?"

Visibly shaken and holding back tears, I turned away from her to answer, "I just got fired." I grabbed my equipment box, looked around for the last time and walked away.

Tears were streaming down my face as I pushed open the door and walked to the parking lot. I opened the trunk of my car and noticed Michelle following me. She could see I was hurting and said, "Come here." She gave me a big hug.

I couldn't hold it back any longer. I sobbed, letting it all out. She held me for a while in front of God and everyone watching. After a few minutes I got in my car and drove home. I never forgot her kindness and compassion during that awful moment.

On the drive home so many thoughts ran through my head. How would I survive? What about my family, the house and the dogs? My career in law enforcement was over, unless I could turn the tide and figure out why my department turned its back on me. They sacrificed a foot soldier to save one of the brass.

But it wasn't enough. Sure, why not kick a man while he's down? San Diego PD continued haunting me in ways large and small for most of the year. It was as if they wanted to keep reminding me, "Don't even think about speaking up." The remainder of this chapter is filled with more dirty tricks they pulled to destroy my life and keep me silenced.

THE KIDS ARE HERE – THEN POOF THEY'RE GONE

Three and a half months later on May 8, 1985 I received a three-page letter* from Attorney Peter M. Polischuk regarding Dissolution/Child Custody and Visitation. My ex-wife followed through with Breitenstein's suggestion to have joint custody of my children removed.

The letter stated he was amicably proposing Susan and I agree to a modification of the current court order concerning child custody and visitation. The basis of the proposal said it was in the best interests of the children due to my circumstances. It read:

"Without unnecessarily elaborating on what concerning your current circumstance has created this need to modify the custody order, suffice it to say because of your present situation regarding the matter under investigation with the Police Department, because of the financial burden and strain this event has placed you under and further because of the additional marital discord between you and your current wife which appears to have been brought on by the investigation and the financial difficulties, the children are better served by shifting responsibility for their primary care to Susan."

"It would appear your present difficult situation is temporary let's face it, we all suffer temporary periods of strain, stress and hard times. Unfortunately, your situation appears to have erupted all at one time. But when difficult times such as those being currently experienced by you also impact upon minor children, steps should be taken to minimize the extent to which the children are affected by the strife. When a reasonable alternative environment for the children is available, such as the one available under Susan's roof, the opportunity to protect the children from unnecessary additional stress should be utilized."

"From the information available to me, I have concluded that the children are definitely showing outward signs of suffering from the present situation. Performance in school is affected and the children have been making comments which would indicate their respective attitudes have taken a turn for the worse as a result of all that surrounds them."

"Therefore, in order to create solutions to the problem that will avoid having to resort to the courts to explain the nature of the problem in greater detail and specificity, I propose the following as a solution which best serves the needs of the children:

The parties stipulate to modify the current custody and visitation order of the court to establish both parties share joint legal custody. This will allow both parties to participate in the important policy-making decisions with respect to health care, education, religious training and the like.

The parties stipulate to modify the court order with regard to primary physical custody causing Susan to be the party with such primary physical responsibility. Primary physical custody would be subject to your having liberal rights of visitation which could either be the subject of a specific visitation schedule or the subject of a flexible general order allowing reasonable visitation. The specifics of a detailed visitation schedule could be worked out with the assistance of the Conciliation Counselor of the Superior Court should you and

Susan require such assistance in the event minor impasses are encountered in working out the specifics between the two of you."

"You should realize Susan's attitude and approach to the proposed modified situation is and will continue to be highly promotive of substantial contact between you and the children. Susan rightly believes such considerable contact is in the best interests of the children and is also beneficial to assisting you in overcoming your temporary situation."

"I am prepared to formulate the stipulation as soon as I receive notice from you that you are willing to go along with the proposal. To reiterate, this voluntary solution to the problem will avoid the spectacle of having to let the courts and the public know further about the details of the current state of affairs. Everyone should agree the children do not need those details to be broadcasted."

"I must insist your response to these proposals be received by my office no later than seven days of the date of this letter, namely, by the end of business on Tuesday, May 14, 1985, otherwise, my client has instructed me to immediately commence a proceeding to effect a change of custody."

"If you have any questions concerning the foregoing, please call. I am more than willing to discuss the matter with you in an effort to achieve what is clearly in everybody's best interests."

Very truly yours,

Peter M. Polischuk

I was backed up against a wall. It felt like extortion of my kids, because I had no money to fight the action. Susan may have done this on her own without Sergeant Breitenstein's prompting. But it was none of his business and he should've butted out.

After the change in custody, things were awfully quiet around the house. No more sounds of my kids laughing and playing. I looked into their empty bedrooms with sadness every time I walked down the hall. It was difficult being alone with just my dogs.

HOW LOW WILL THE SHERIFF'S DEPARTMENT STOOP?

The San Diego Sheriff's Department was in a frenzy to solve the Donna Gentile murder. Laws were broken to obtain evidence. There was too much media attention and he wanted a quick solution to the murder with an arrest.

In October 1985, I was contacted by Detective Tom Streed, the lead investigator on the Gentile murder while at my mother-in-law's home. He wanted to talk with me at the Sheriff's Department, but only if I'd come in without an attorney. I told him I'd come in, but it was my right to be represented by counsel. I knew if I went down there, I'd never leave.

Streed said, "Then I don't want to talk to you." He called Connie Zimmerman, one of my former Sergeants. They discussed the possibility of her trying to talk me into coming in without an attorney. Streed told Zimmerman not to discuss their conversation with me. Instead, Connie called me immediately.

In September of 1985 my ex-wife and her new husband took the kids to Seattle. He was in the Navy and worked on submarines. Between September and November of 1985, it was just me and my three Bassett hounds, Holly, Polly and her daddy, Schroeder. * They were great dogs. I wish I still had them today. They were so unconditionally loving and affectionate. I would take them everywhere with me. Sometimes I wouldn't eat for days just so I had gas in the car and food for my dogs. Life was a personal hell.

GARY KENDRICK FRIEND THEN FOE

As a kid, I amassed a sizeable and valuable comic book collection. As an adult one place where I bought comics was Wonder City Comics in Santee, California.

The owner was Gary Kendrick. He also had a mail order comic business and he dabbled in real estate.

In 1983, when I was living in Santee and working for the police department I'd stop by his store and became a regular customer. We became friendly and on February 18, 1983 Kendrick went on a Ride-A-Long with me.* He enjoyed the experience and wrote notes about what he observed. Kendrick wrote he was amazed how I could multi-task, drive a patrol car, watch traffic, look for reasons to pull someone over, listen to the radio and carry on a conversation all at the same time.

I listened to him talk about how lucrative the comic book business was. He explained it as a low to no overhead business, with a steady weekly cash flow. One time he showed me a bank deposit book and I saw hundreds of dollars being deposited weekly.

I inquired what it would take to start a business like his.

Kendrick replied, "As a matter of fact I'm thinking about selling my business and selling off my collection by mail order. The numbers looked good and I told him I might be interested, but I couldn't put any money down.

Kendrick said, "What about the deed to your house?"

I said, "I can't risk the house. What if the business failed?"

He reminded me about his books with all the deposits. If I ever needed financial assistance, he'd help he told me.

How could I go wrong? I thought about it for a week and agreed to the deal.

Comic books are ordered three months in advance and you must estimate whether a book will be a great seller or just average. Sometimes I'd order more than I needed, and a book would bomb. Or I'd be too conservative, and a popular book would sell out early. If I couldn't get any more, a customer might go elsewhere to get what I didn't have in stock and I'd lose a customer. There were about four competitors in town.

To prevent this from happening, I put a plan in action with the other comic book stores. Instead of working against them, I offered to help if they were short on issues. They did the same, so we kept our customers happy and didn't lose clientele.

The first three months after taking over, Kendrick insisted on ordering until I got the hang of it. After six months I figured Kendrick overordered everything. I was stuck with product I couldn't sell. It was like stapling a dollar bill to every book I was stuck with. Even after I took over ordering I was behind.

On a weekly basis, business was good. But it reached a point where I couldn't order enough of what I needed. The orders cost so much with the glut of books, games, dice and lead figures for gaming it became difficult to compete. Two years after buying the business, I sought financial help from Kendrick in late March of 1985 once I was no longer working for the department.

Kendrick denied ever agreeing to help me.

The owner of the jewelry store next door came over and told me along with an ex-employee of Kendrick's, he boasted about showing me a different set of books before I bought the business. He had showed me deposits from his rental tenants, not from the comic book store. I accused Kendrick of defrauding me and told him I'd seek legal recourse.

Later that day I received a call from Sergeant Greg Clark from Internal Affairs saying Kendrick filed a complaint saying I attempted to extort money from him. Kendrick thought he could get my house faster by attempting to add a criminal charge.

Why was Internal Affairs still in my life? Was it purely to harass me? I told Clark I was no longer on the department and to leave me alone. "You can shove your allegations," I said and hung up. Apparently, the call was just to harass me because I never heard from them again.

Kendrick filed foreclosure papers through his attorney and I lost my house to him on November 18,1985. The Sheriff and the Marshal came out to make sure I vacated the premises.

He became a Councilman for the City of El Cajon and was a politician until recently. His most recent position was Mayor pro tem and his term expired in December 2018.

The day I moved out of the house, my 1977 Datsun F-10 was parked in my driveway and inoperable. I moved it to the street and asked the Sheriff's Deputy if I could leave it legally parked on Via Rita. The Deputy said it would be okay for a couple days. I was driving a moving van full of my possessions, plus I had two cars to drive out of the area. I moved my 1980 Ford Mustang to my friend's house where I would spend the night.

My friend, Tom Hofius was a Postal Inspector. He couldn't believe what the city was doing.

The Datsun wasn't operating due to a sparkplug problem. With no money coming in, I couldn't afford get the problem fixed or tow the car. The registration tags were also expired, and I couldn't afford to update them either.

The day after moving, I returned. My car was missing from where I parked it. I called the Sheriff's Department to see if it was stolen.

The dispatcher told me it wasn't stolen, it was impounded.

I asked impounded per what section.

I was told Section 22651(o) of the vehicle code.

I became upset with the dispatcher because Section 22651(o)vc states to impound a vehicle the registration must be expired at least a year and a day; it must have five outstanding parking tickets and must be a hazard. It wasn't expired a year and a day; it didn't have five outstanding tickets and it was properly parked and not a hazard.

I called the California Highway Patrol and spoke to Sergeant John Mc Donald. I used to meet with him off the freeway. He oversaw training and, if anyone knew the vehicle code backward and forward, it was John. He felt the county had no grounds to tow the vehicle.

I called the Sheriff's dispatcher and asked where the vehicle was impounded.

She said it was at Fletcher Hills Towing in El Cajon, a few miles away.

I asked her if there were any holds on the vehicle.

After a long silence she finally replied, "You'll have to ask Fletcher Hills Towing." I knew something was up. The dispatcher wasn't telling me everything.

I called Fletcher Hills Towing to talk with their dispatcher.

The dispatcher referred me to the manager who told me there was a hold on the vehicle, but he couldn't tell me what it was. He referred me back to the Sheriff.

I'd had enough of the bureaucratic shuffle and told the manager, "Look idiot, can you read? What does it say on my windshield, or do I have to come down there with an attorney and start flinging lawsuits left and right?"

The manager said, "Okay, it says hold for homicide."

A cold chill came over me, which quickly turned into rage. I thought, they think I killed her. Those jerks were barking up the wrong tree.

I calmed down and called the Santee Sheriff's Substation and asked to speak to the detective who handled vehicle impounds. I was connected to Detective Willouby. I told him who I was and asked him why my vehicle was towed.

Willouby told me he had the report. He read Deputy Blu's report to me. The officer wrote while on patrol in the 9800 block of Via Rita, she spotted a vehicle that was 4000(A)vc expired registration in violation of Section 22651(o)vc. She called senior traffic officer Wong to the scene and impounded the vehicle.

Officer Ed Wong used to buy comic books from me. I called him at home and asked about my vehicle being impounded.

He replied, "I got a call to meet Deputy Blu at your address regarding the impounding of a vehicle. When I arrived, I recognized your car and saw your uniform shirt with the nametag inside. Blu told me she received a call from Sheriff's homicide to get my car any way you can. Blu asked me if she could impound it per that section. I told her no and left the scene."

There was no record of this conversation in the impound report, which means the report was false. Deputy Blu wasn't on patrol near my house. She was directed there by Sheriff's homicide. I was beginning to see how the Sheriff's Department ran their homicide investigations.

I called Detective Willouby back and asked to speak to his boss.

Willouby said his boss was Lieutenant Swink.

I spoke to Swink and he said he could release the car to me if he wanted to, but he didn't want to. If I came up with half of the money to pay the impound fee, the Sheriff would take care of the rest. Knowing I couldn't pay even half the charges, it was an empty offer.

My next call was to Lieutenant Bill Baxter, from the Sheriff's homicide division to ask why he impounded my car.

Baxter said he didn't know what I was talking about.

I was so tired of being played. I said, "Bullshit! I'm a cop, remember. I'm not some John Q. Public. I know how the system works. You're the head of the Homicide unit, you're responsible for the actions of the officers in your command. You either told Streed to impound my vehicle, he asked you if he could impound it or he told you he was impounding it!!"

My vehicle was impounded for evidence, but the report was full of false statements and omissions to skirt around the law.

I had to store my things and board my three Bassett hounds in Ramona, California, a city 25 miles away. Before my kids were born, my dogs were my "kids." They've all passed on, but they were a true source of comfort back in those difficult days. Especially after losing custody of my kids who then left California.

VIOLATING OUR FIRST AMENDMENT RIGHT TO ASSEMBLE

In December 1985, a group of former officers met at Sy Casady's house. Casady formerly published the Arizona Republic, the major daily newspaper in Phoenix and throughout Arizona. In 1985, he published The Daily Californian, a San Diego newspaper published four days a week with a circulation of 30,000 papers daily.

Casady was close friends with former US Congressman Lionel Van Deerlin. Van Deerlin wrote a column in the San Diego Union Tribune. He wanted to send in sworn statements from these former police officers to Congress asking for an investigation into repeated reports of cover-ups and corruption within the San Diego Police Department.

While meeting at Casady's home it became apparent we were under surveillance by the Criminal Intelligence Unit.

We reported it to the F.B.I. and were told they were aware of the department's activity. They explained it this way, "Imagine you're being watched from a hill looking down on you. Now imagine us above them looking down from another hill at them watching you."

I wanted to understand the department's reasons? Why were they worried about being so squeaky clean?

We got our statements to Congressman Jim Bates who forwarded them to Congress.*

CHAPTER THIRTEEN

SURVIVING THE MEAN STREETS

I NEVER THOUGHT FEEDING my kids and taking care of them would be difficult until I lost my job with the police department. After my termination effective January 22, 1985, I worked a myriad of jobs. At this point I still owned my comic book store, located at 9315 Mission Gorge Road, across the street from KCBQ Radio.

I kept the business until April 1985 when I could no longer pay the rent. I was lucky though, my landlord Roy Woodward, a City Councilman for the City of Santee allowed me to break the lease after I explained my situation to him. I got a large moving van and with the help of my postal inspector friend we moved the contents of my store into the living room of my house. It was about a mile and a half away from the store. I had a large, 20 x 20-foot living room. It would have to be big to accommodate two book shelves, ten feet long and eight feet tall. With few exceptions this worked out quite well. During this time, it was my only source of income.

My plan was to connect my business phone into a jack in my house and hook up my answering machine with a recorded message of what comic books would arrive the coming week. Customers would leave messages requesting the books they wanted. When I got home, I'd play back the messages, write down the orders and pull each order individually from my inventory on the big shelves in the living room. After totaling each order I'd drive to their home to collect their money. This was effective from April of 1985 until November; however, it wasn't generating enough cash flow, so our house went into foreclosure. I was served with a kick out order* from the Marshal's Office.

Most of my deliveries were done on Friday night, Saturday mornings and Sunday morning. One customer was a teen of 15 or 16, by the name of Frank Hilliker. His father owned an egg ranch in Santee and it was nothing for him to buy $50.00 to $60.00 dollars' worth of comics every week. When things got tough, I could usually count on a phone call from Frank. He'll never know how many times his comic book purchases put food on my table.

When it came to feeding my kids and pets, I often went hungry, so they had food to eat. If I had a few bucks, I'd buy one of those huge pizzas which barely fit in my car and we'd eat pizza for several days. I also made what I called "Larry's Poor Man Spaghetti." It included whatever pasta I had with minced garlic, butter and tossed with parmesan cheese. It was satisfying and my kids loved it. I always made sure there was fresh fruit at home. Jim from the 7-Eleven® store on one of my old beats gave me fresh fruit every week. If I received a lot of money, I'd let some of the house bills go and stock the house with groceries. When I stocked the house with food, I made sure my kids and I ate balanced, healthy meals and snacks. Things were tough but we survived. Despite the enormous pressure I was under, I couldn't let the department win.

In April of 1985, I got a job working building security at 939 Coast Boulevard in La Jolla. Bing Crosby's brother Bob lived there. It wasn't much of a job, but it helped pay the bills.

My boss was Lou Chatelle. He lived in San Carlos and when I interviewed for the job, I told him the whole story. I mentioned if he checked with the city, he wouldn't get a favorable reply. Chatelle told me he'd do me one better. He lived down the street from a Sergeant from the San Diego Police Department. I asked him who it was, but he wouldn't say.

Lou said, "I'll ask my neighbor about you and see what he says. A few days later I got the job. I found out where my new boss lived and checked with the County Assessor's Office. The only person on Chatelle's street who was in the department was Sergeant Ramsey. As a Reserve officer I worked with Ramsey's downtown squad. Ramsey must've said I was okay because I got the job. It's simple, if you do well, people remember. If you screw up, people remember as well.

I held the job as a corporate security officer for just a few months until July 10, 1985. The building manager felt I was too controversial for residents to read about me in the newspaper, see my picture on television then see me in the lobby. Of course, I was told the building was cutting back on staff to make their budget. I had to go because I was the junior man.

Once again, I was out of work and surviving on the income from my comic book business. The next day was my birthday. Happy Birthday, Larry! Nothing good to celebrate.

I didn't find work until September when I started working for a former police officer. Suzie Shertz ran a construction cleanup business where new apartment units were being built in University City. We cleaned up the drywall scraps, get paint off the windows, remove all the trash and get the units ready for tenants to move in.

One night after work I forgot to buy dog food at the feed store. I was exhausted from working and just wanted to get home. So, I stopped at a 7-Eleven® store up the street from my house. It was Halloween night, and never did I imagine I'd be pressed into service to help stop a thief. A large man working on his car in the parking lot was talking to two women. He was shirtless, flexing his muscles for them and kissing his biceps as I passed him on my way inside. Apparently, trying to impress them he entered the store, walked immediately back to the cooler, removed two 12-packs of beer and preceded to walk out of the store without paying. The store was packed full of customers in line waiting to pay.

When he walked out, the store clerk said, "Did you see that? He just stole beer. Somebody stop him."

I put the dog food bag down, walked outside and over to him and the two women. While he was talking to them and bragging about what he did, I reached over, grabbed the two 12-packs and started walking back toward the store.

He shouted at me and said, "Hey asshole, bring back my beer!"

I replied it wasn't his because he didn't pay for it.

He shouted again and said, "Hey asshole bring my beer back now, or I'm gonna rip your head off and shit down your neck."

It sounded like fighting words to me. He started advancing toward me and took a swing. I ducked under and placed him in a carotid (sleeper hold) restraint which rendered him unconscious. I dragged him back into the 7-Eleven®, turned him over and placed my knee behind his neck. I instructed the clerk to call the Sheriff and tell them I was holding someone in custody for theft. The customers burst into applause and cheers and began kicking him on their way out. I shouted to them he was under control and asked them not to kick him. The first Sheriff's car to respond was a traffic unit. I looked up as the officer walked in the store and our eyes locked.

"Happy Halloween Larry," he said. It was Bill Fitzgerald, who I carpooled with when I was in the police academy. He laterally trans-

ferred from our department to the Sheriff's department after graduation. It was like old home week.

The arrest made Tom Blair's column* in the San Diego Union that
week. Even though I wasn't a cop anymore, I could still feel it
coursing through my veins. It was still in my blood and it was exhil-
arating.

I held my job with Suzie until the foreclosure resulted in me being
forcibly evicted from my house. Because of the stress on my wife, we
decided she'd move back in with her folks until she could get her
brittle diabetes under control.

When it was time to move out of my house, twelve terrific officers
from the department helped me jam everything I owned into my
1977 Datsun F-10 (which was later impounded), my 1980 Ford
Mustang and the 24-foot U-Haul® truck I rented.

I rented a storage space in Spring Valley years ago to store the
contents of my comic book store and my personal collection. This is
where I stored the contents of my home.

The house I had to walk away from was over 1400 square feet with a
two-car attached garage, a country kitchen, covered patio, a 20x20
living room, four bedrooms and two full bathrooms.

There was so much I left behind. I sold my new barbecue and lawn-
mower to my next-door neighbors for $150.00. I loved to cook, and the
kitchen was complete with every appliance and gadget you could
imagine from a donut/bagel maker to a crepe maker and Tandoori clay
cooking pots. Before moving out, I cut the cords off all the appliances
and left them in the cabinets. I couldn't take them with me, and I didn't
want the person who repossessed my place to have them either. I left a
King size water bed with high rails and cabinets, a bookshelf with a large
inset mirror. I left a five-blade ceiling fan with light kit above my bed. I
also left behind all my training materials from the Police Academy.

There was barely enough room for two of the three dogs in large animal crates in the back seat. The third went up with me in the cab of the truck. I parked my Ford Mustang at a friend's house in San Carlos.

The next day, I moved into my in-law's house where my wife was living. If there was ever a hotter place then hell, this was it. My father-in-law was an old, crotchety man with old attitudes. If you were a Democrat, he liked you. If you possessed more money than he did, he didn't like you. He was a retired union carpenter who didn't like anyone who was unlicensed or not a union man. He came from an old German family. Naturally, being Jewish didn't score any points for me, either. The rent was $60.00 a week.

My parents never really knew the total devastation of what happened. They knew I lost jobs in the past, but they figured I was resourceful and would find another job. They never asked if I needed money or help and I never asked them for anything.

I started thinking about my options in life. I could move back to Illinois and live with my parents rent free and start over. The thought was there because my mother was diagnosed with Multiple Sclerosis and was wheelchair bound. But I wasn't brought up to run and take the easy way out. I was raised to stand up and fight for what was right and never quit, no matter what the odds. The San Diego Police Department simply didn't understand this about me.

They expected me to fold under pressure, commit suicide or turn to crime to survive and eventually get caught, so they could tell the world how right they were. But I decided to stay and fight and to become a success in their own backyard. Success and living well is the best revenge.

I always made a point of shaking hands with anyone from the opposition, just to let them know I was still around, and I wasn't quitting.

I remember one person saying to me, "I thought you were dead."

Dick Weber, a reporter for the San Diego Union did a story one year after my hearing. In the article I was quoted saying, "I'm never giving up. The department will eat, sleep and breathe Avrech."

In December of 1985, I started working for a telemarketing firm called American Life. They were in the Kearny Mesa area not far from my in-law's house. The business sold coupon books over the phone. Once a sale was made, the phone salesperson would drive out, collect the money and deliver the book to the customer.

One day I made a sale and a delivery to a middle-age woman. Her apartment was somewhere in the Kensington area. I knew the area and worked it as a Police Officer. When I arrived, I noticed her gray hair in a ponytail and welcoming smile. She opened the door and looked at me through my smile and said, "Child, you look troubled, please come in."

I was puzzled and told her I could accept a check or cash for her coupon book.

She walked over to me with a Bible in her hand and said, "Here take this Bible and whenever you feel like you're being unjustly attacked, you read these two Psalms and they'll protect you from evil."

They were Psalm 7 and Psalm 54. I tried to tell her I couldn't accept the Bible from her but she wouldn't take no for an answer and practically pushed me out of her apartment with it.* I got in my car and felt like a huge weight lifted off my shoulders. I tried to analyze what just occurred.

Was she a Psychic, could she read my mind? Or, was she an Angel of God sent to help? Every night, before I went to bed, I'd recite the Psalms. Whenever I was feeling down, I'd pick it up and read those two Psalms again. I found them comforting and they helped ease my stress a bit. A few of the lines most helpful to me were:

Psalms 7 said, 1: "O Lord my God, in you I put my trust; Save me from all those who persecute me; and deliver me,

2: Lest they tear me like a lion, rending me in pieces, while there is none to deliver.

3: O Lord my God, If I have done this: If there is iniquity in my hands

4: If I have repaid evil to him who was at peace with me or have plundered my enemy without cause,

5: Let the enemy pursue me and overtake me; yes, let him trample my life to the earth and lay my honor in the dust. Selah

6: Arise, O Lord, In your anger; Lift yourself up because of the rage of my enemies,

And awake for me to the Judgment you have commanded.

8: Judge me O Lord, according to my righteousness, and according to my integrity within me.

9: Oh, let the wickedness of the wicked come to an end, but establish the just;

14: Behold, the wicked travails with iniquity, conceives trouble and brings forth falsehood.

15: He made a pit and dug it out and has fallen into the ditch which he made.

16: His trouble shall return upon his own head and his violent dealing shall come down on his own crown."

Psalm 54 said, 1: "Save me O God, by your name, and vindicate me by your strength.

2: Hear my Prayer, O God; Give ear to the words of my mouth.

3: For strangers have risen up against me, and oppressors have sought after my life; they have not set God before them. Selah

4: Behold, God is my helper; The Lord is with those who uphold my life.

5: He will repay my enemies for their evil; cut them off in your truth.

7: For he has delivered me out of all trouble; and my eye has seen its desire upon my enemies.

Oh, how these lines from the Bible she insisted I have, paralleled my plight. I prayed for help and eventually my prayers were answered.

In January of 1986, I was working for a security company, Columbia Security doing Internal Investigations for the company. I was supposed to be making $1200.00 a month. The company filed bankruptcy and my paycheck went to cover his wedding in Las Vegas. The owner John S. Goulart was skimming money off the top and not paying payroll taxes. I never got paid. I took Goulart to small claims court and prevailed, but the Judgement was stayed when he filed bankruptcy.

The following day, I went to my attorney, Don Peterson and asked him if I could do any work for him. Peterson started me off serving legal papers. This started to snowball in the office when his partner Tony Caputo also gave me papers to serve. Caputo's wife Kathryn was also an attorney in another law office with seven other attorneys. I was making $20.00 on each paper served. I was serving 10-12 papers a week and started putting money away.

The serving of papers became harder to accomplish. People were expecting them. They would lie to your face and be evasive. I decided to find ways to beat them at their own game. I was charging more now, but I was getting the job done. I opened a process serving business called "Larry's Carry." Business was pretty good. If I came to the door with a bouquet of flowers for a woman, they would always open their door. For the guys it was an empty pizza box. If I wanted a certain person to come out from their house to me, I'd take the want ads from the newspaper with the papers inside and start walking around the person's vehicle and look inside until I was spotted. I got them to come to me, thinking I was somehow tampering with their vehicle and when they least expected it, GOTCHA!

While I was doing pretty well, I was contacted by a server in Orange County. It was becoming cost prohibitive for him to send someone down to San Diego to serve his papers. I arranged for him to mail them to me and split the cost of the services. I did this for about a year and made some pretty good money on a volume basis.

I lived at my in-laws until February of 1986 when I was told I couldn't stay there any longer. I mean, I was still married but I needed to find another place. My wife Paula, knew friends in the rabbit breeding business who lived on the other side of town in Lemon Grove.

My animals were well taken care of free of charge in a kennel in Ramona about 25 miles away. So, I picked up as much stuff as I could and moved to Bernice and her brother Burt Dilley's house. Bernice told me I could live in Burt's 33-foot motorhome. It contained a Queen size bed, bathroom and shower, sink and stove. All the comforts of home, except I didn't have a home anymore.

I needed to find another career and at the same time, I needed a diversion so I wouldn't spend all my time on the phone discussing my case. I was obsessed with solving the case, putting the blame where it rightfully belonged and vindicating myself, but how?

On February 12, 1986, I went to the courthouse downtown to do some research. I forgot it was a court holiday and the courts and offices were closed. I wondered if the District Attorney's Office was open. I went up to the fourth floor to see if I could find Guy Johnson. Guy used to be a San Diego Police Officer and worked Eastern

Division. He was now an investigator for the District Attorney's Office.

It was a known fact, there was a connection between Johnson and Donna Gentile. Every time Gentile was stopped on the street and asked for her driver's license, she would thumb through cards in her wallet and would pass a card from the police department with Guy Johnson's name on it. Johnson also played a role in a companion investigation regarding my case with my Sergeant Connie Zimmerman. You may recall, it was Zimmerman I went to after finding out my Lieutenant Carl Black was taking Gentile to the Colorado River for a weekend. Johnson was a player somehow and I needed to know what he knew regarding Gentile and the Investigation. I found Johnson was in and started asking him questions.

Johnson told me, "I can't talk to you it's too political. In order for me to talk to you I would have to talk with my boss, Ed Miller, the District Attorney and he would have to talk to the Police Department and get their permission so I could talk to you."

Later the same day I was followed all over San Diego by Detectives from the special investigation's unit of the police department. First, when you follow someone it's a good idea to use people the target won't recognize. I made enough right turns and pulled over enough times as they drove by several times. This was a joke!

Why was I followed? Who made a phone call? Johnson? If so, why? Why me? What did they stand to gain by harassing me? This was more harassment at its best.

Things didn't work out at my new place with the Dilley's. They were kind, lovely people. However, because of my irregular schedule I'd get back late, and they would be waiting with supper for me. I appreciated everything they did, but I couldn't adapt to their lifestyle. So once again I was homeless.

I contacted Doug Seymour, a former police Reserve Officer, who worked undercover and infiltrated the Ku Klux Klan. He was asked to interfere with Tom Metzger's political campaign for US Congress. This was in violation of the Hatch act, but when Seymour sued the city, they denied any culpability or responsibility. When the Klan found out he was a plant and played Russian Roulette with him for hours, Seymour suffered a mental breakdown. Another example of the Department turning its back on one of their own.

Seymour owned a construction business, San Diego Building and Development. His partner was Rod Quigley one of my old Sergeants. I also worked an undercover narcotics assignment for Quigley when he ran the Ocean Beach drug sweeps back when I was a Reserve Officer.*

Doug gave me a job and a place to live. He lived in a magnificent house in the hills of Escondido on Mary Lane. I lived in a small studio, connected to the main house by a long stairwell. This used to be Doug's home office where he drew up house plans. I felt like I was living in the Batcave when Doug would call me upstairs for dinner. I'd drive Doug to work in his car and saved wear and tear on my Mustang. While at work, I was a laborer and did odd jobs like nailing roofs. I learned how to hang sheetrock and carry it properly. I was working hard and probably in great shape physically, tipping the scales at 169. But mentally, I wasn't there. I remember being totally preoccupied at a jobsite thinking about the department and how they let me down. My thoughts meandered to how I lost my job, lost my house, my wife, my kids, my dogs. I'd suddenly go into crying jags for no apparent reason. I didn't know why, and I couldn't help myself. Sometimes television would help me fall asleep. I'd turn it on and start watching something and before I knew it, I'd be asleep. One night I experienced a strange phenomenon at Doug's house. CBS used to have a late show on television staring Charlie Rose as the host. I remember looking at the clock while watching the program which would repeat in several hours and then I'd wake up several nights in a row at the same time, I last watched the same interview. It seemed as if time was standing still, like I was in limbo or some sort of time warp.

My life was mostly on hold. I had a roof over my head and food to eat, but I wasn't happy and half of my paychecks bounced. Doug's business was in big trouble and I never knew whether my check would clear the bank or bounce.

In May of 1986, Doug told me I'd have to find another place to live because he made arrangements for someone from the church who needed a place to stay. Doug's two sons also worked for him and it was suggested I look for a place to live with them. They found a place in Escondido. I stayed there one month before moving back to my in-law's house. Apparently, Paula was feeling much better and wanted to try again. From July of 1986 to August of 1988 I moved back in.

These experiences made it difficult for me to trust people for a long time. What I thought was a sure thing would turn into a sham over and over. The plans and goals I'd set for myself not only weren't happening, but I felt I kept going backward, barely surviving.

CHAPTER FOURTEEN

MY LIFESAVERS

THERE ARE many types of Life Savers in this world. Some are thrown by lifeguards to save a person from drowning. Some are used to freshen one's breath or ease a queasy stomach. But I needed life savers to save my life and my future. The good Lord provided them to me.

As I wrote this chapter, I found I wasn't just retelling the events that occurred to me and my family, I was reliving it at the same time. At times, I had to put the material aside and go on and write other chapters which were less emotional.

Rich Bonin, a reporter and head producer at 60 Minutes and his producer at the time Lowell Bergman received a letter* forwarded from CBS reporter Mike Wallace. The letter was typed by my former wife Susan who was briefed by my current wife, Paula. I was under strict orders not to discuss my case with anyone but my attorney, my wife and members of Internal Affairs. My current wife Paula was under no such order. The letter requested their help with my situation and the department. It was sent by Federal Express to them in November of 1985.*

Bergman did an expose' regarding the Yellow Cab Scandal of 1970 in San Diego, where the Mayor, Frank Curran and seven city councilmen were indicted and charged with bribery and conspiracy to grant a 1967 fare increase to the Yellow Cab Company after receiving contributions from the owner,* The Police Chief also received a new car every year.

Named in the indictment besides the Mayor were council members Alan Hitch, Mike Schaeffer, Floyd Morrow, Helen Cobb and former members Tom Hom, Harry Scheidle and Jack Walsh. Hitch pleaded no contest to a reduced misdemeanor charge, while the others were ultimately either acquitted or the charges against them were dropped.

When Bergman read my letter he said, "Looks like San Diego is up to their old tricks. We'll have to go back to San Diego again and see what's up." Bergman sent his right-hand man, Rich Bonin to see me.

By the time Bonin arrived at my store the following month. I no longer was under the order "not to discuss this matter." I couldn't wait to spill my guts. After speaking with him I was told to contact a local newspaper reporter I could trust. I was given the name of Jon Standefer of the San Diego Union.

I found Standefer listed in the phone book and called him.

He said, "I'd like to run your story and it's not that we don't believe you, but before we print anything would you be willing to take a polygraph exam?"

I said, "Sure, but I can't afford it."

Standefer said, "That's okay don't worry about the expense, the owner of the newspaper, will pay for it." Standefer told me to meet him for lunch in La Jolla at the Marine Room.

At this point in my life, I couldn't afford to wash dishes at the Marine Room let alone eat off them. The restaurant was just off the ocean with breathtaking views. * The newspaper went to the expense because they believed in me. Jon was a tall well-tanned man wearing a Hawaiian shirt, white pants and a straw calypso-type hat. I was expecting someone in a three-piece suit. But, if he could help me, I wouldn't have cared if he wore shorts and sandals.

We discussed my case over lunch. Jon gave me the name Donald Hardy, a local polygrapher. Standefer used him before and was very pleased with his expertise. Hardy was located in the Clairemont area. His office was in a building at the corner of Balboa and Genesee Avenue. The date for the polygraph was scheduled for January 17, 1986 at 10:40 am.

I walked into Hardy's office. It was dimly lit with a nightstand table and a few chairs in the waiting room. There was no receptionist. I took a seat and waited. I was excited, anxious and a little fearful. But I knew I told the truth and I had nothing to do with Gentile's death. It was eerily quiet.

Suddenly, I heard a door open and shut. Here stood a man in his 50's with black salt and pepper grey hair and about five-foot eight inches tall. He sported a welcoming grin on his face.

He introduced himself as Donald Hardy, a Private Investigator and Polygraph examiner who was a retired Homicide Sergeant with the San Bernardino Sheriff's department.

There was that word again, "Homicide." It never bothered me before, but it did now. I felt like I was on the inside looking out even though I knew I had done nothing wrong.

Hardy shook my hand and said, "Come on back."

My heart was racing fast enough inside to fill a traffic officer's ticket book. I kept saying to myself, "Calm down, everything will be okay."

Hardy obtained some history from me, but he already spoke with Standefer. Hardy explained the testing procedure and told me he wouldn't ask any question we hadn't discussed.

Prior to the actual test Hardy put me through a "coin test" to show me just how sensitive and accurate the polygraph was. Hardy placed four coins down in the outer office. Once he returned, he told me to go in the outer office and pick up one of the coins either a penny, nickel, dime or quarter and put it in my pocket.

I wasn't to tell Hardy which coin I took.

Hardy would hook me up to the polygraph machine and ask me questions as to whether I picked up a penny, a nickel, a dime or a quarter. He instructed me to answer "no" to all the questions and on the answer regarding the question about the coin I took.

I understood and he began the test.

He said, "Larry, did you pick up the penny?"

I replied, "No."

He said, "Larry, did you pick up the nickel?"

I replied, "No."

He said, Larry, did you pick up the dime?"

I replied, "No."

He said, Larry, did you pick up the quarter?"

I replied, "No."

Hardy turned off the machine and told me to relax. He looked at the chart and said, "Larry give me my nickel."

I reached in my pocket and produced his nickel I picked up. I thought to myself, wow, the machine was extremely sensitive, and it caught me when I lied. I felt much more relaxed knowing the machine would show me telling the truth. We went over the test questions once again.

Hardy said he was going to administer what is called a "SKY" test.

Hardy explained the letters S K and Y were acronyms for, do you suspect, do you know, and did you kill Donna Marie Gentile.

I requested my department give me a polygraph test against the good advice of my attorney, but they wouldn't. They never tested Gentile because it would've blown the department's whole case against me. As George Varela from the Chief's office said, "It fit the specific needs of the department at that particular time."

Hardy tested me several times. When the test was complete, Hardy took the galvanic skin response device off my fingers, released the air from the tube around my chest and the cuff from my arm and turned off the machine. He leaned forward with his hands interlaced together in front of him on his desk and said, "I've been a Homicide Investigator for many years and have interrogated and interviewed hundreds if not thousands of people for possible involvement in crimes. I can tell you with 100 percent certainty you had nothing to do with the Gentile murder."

I broke out in a big smile on my face as tears welled up in my eyes. I knew I was innocent of any wrongdoing, but now I had confirmation from an expert.*

If not for 60 Minutes I would never have met Jon Standefer. And, if not for Jon Standefer I would never have met Don Hardy. Sadly, in September of 2017, Jon the lynchpin and the force behind my case going forward succumbed to cancer. He was planning on writing the Foreword to this book. Rest in Peace Jon, you were a Life Saver.

Don Hardy and I stayed in touch and became best of friends. He also played a pivotal role in my case. Don and I would meet occasionally for lunch. He became busy with pre-employment testing and testing homicide suspects with the Fontana Police department. He turned his local San Diego caseload over to me once I received my P.I. license.

JOHN MORRISON

Back in the mid 70's before becoming a Police Officer, I worked for the former Chief of Police, Raymond Hoobler. After leaving the department Hoobler became head of security for the Atlas Hotels in San Diego. The Atlas Hotels also owned hotel properties in Los Angeles and in Scottsdale, Arizona. Hoobler ran his staff like a second police department.

The hotel properties in San Diego were in the Hotel Circle area off Interstate 8 in Mission Valley. They were the Town and Country, the Mission Valley Inn, the King's Inn, the Ramada Inn and the Hanalei. They were all in a circle on both sides of the freeway.

Because of the crime in the area involving robberies, car prowls, stolen vehicles and prostitution, we had constant patrol from the San Diego Police Department. Before decentralization the Hotel Circle area was covered by the Northern Division. In 1976 I met and became friends with John Morrison. He was one of the Sergeants assigned to the area. His units would stop into the coffee shop to eat, finish their reports, have coffee or meet the Sergeant to sign their reports.

We've remained friends to this day. John verified my 6000 hours of investigative time while on the department which qualified me for my 1988 Private Investigator's license. He kept me abreast of happenings on the department and assisted me in cases I worked.

Years later, John moved to Driggs, Idaho and became their City Manager for several years. Occasionally, he and his wife Nancy would make trips back to San Diego. Her parents lived in San Diego and I'd meet them for dinner. John was a great speaker and was asked to speak at an F.B.I. academy graduation.

In the 90's John was contacted for comment from the Oceanside Blade Newspaper They did an article about me.* Morrison said, "No one short of an innocent man would torture himself the way Larry did. Over the years Larry did nothing more than push for a more far-reaching investigation. He wanted all the skeleton's exposed."

Thanks John, for being there for me when I needed you. You were a lifesaver.

RICHARD (DICK) J. LEWIS

In the spring of 1986, I was living at my in-law's house behind the Eastern Division sub-station in Serra Mesa when Don Hardy called me.

Hardy said he went out for dinner last night with one of his old bosses from the San Bernardino Sheriff's Department. He went on to tell me he worked under him in Homicide. He was also a former Lieutenant in Criminal Intelligence. His name was Richard (Dick) Lewis, older brother to US Congressman Jerry Lewis (R) from Redlands, California.

Dick was on loan years ago to the San Diego District Attorney's office during the Yellow Cab Scandal. The District Attorney needed someone whose face was unknown in San Diego during the Investigation. After the investigation was completed, Dick picked up stakes and moved to San Diego to take on his new job as a full-time investigator for the D.A.'s office. During this time, he attended Law School and became a Deputy District Attorney. Lewis moved up quickly within the organization and was well-liked by the upper crust.

Hardy told me the subject of last night's dinner was my case. Lewis followed the case quite closely and wondered if I'd be willing to discuss it with him. Hardy gave me his number and said Lewis was assigned to special operations. Spec Ops was a division of the District Attorney's Office which handled complex cases involving politicians, police officers and organized crime.

I called his office but couldn't reach him this time. After a little phone tag, Lewis returned my call. He spoke in a low, deep voice.

Lewis said, "Larry, I know you were set up by your department and I can prove it. Would you be willing to come down to my office tomorrow morning about 10:00 and talk with me?"

I couldn't believe what I just heard. I almost choked on my tongue. Here was a high-ranking deputy district attorney in a position of authority, telling me he could prove I was set up. Were my prayers finally answered?

Lewis said, "Tiger, you don't have a sour grapes story."

I asked Lewis if I needed to bring him any documentation.

Lewis said, "No, not yet."

I hung up and couldn't believe what I just heard. I looked up as if I could see through the ceiling to the sky above. I was trying to comprehend the conversation. Would he get me my job back? Exactly what did this mean? I couldn't think straight. I was in a daze. I was counting the seconds. I couldn't wait to meet with this man.

I sat awake all night just repeating his words over and over in my mind.

"You were set up and I can prove it!!"

I couldn't fall asleep that night. Tomorrow wouldn't come soon enough for me. It was as if time stood still. I thought of one of my sayings I made up. "Failure is immediate, but success is always at a snail's pace" At some time I finally fell asleep and the next thing I knew, it was morning. But it was only 5: 45 am. I didn't dare go back to sleep and take a chance I might oversleep and miss my appointment.

I watched the news, ate breakfast, shaved showered and got dressed. I looked at the clock in the kitchen and it was only 8:00 am. Still another two more hours before I had to be there. Time was moving in slow motion. I couldn't wait for 10:00 am to roll around.

It took 25 minutes figuring on traffic, to drive downtown and find a parking place. The suspense was killing me. I took four pens and a new writing tablet with me. I was going to be an intelligent listener and write like the wind.

Driving through traffic seemed like everyone was moving except me. I couldn't wait to arrive fast enough. Finally, I pulled in at the Wells Fargo Bank Building downtown where some of the District Attorney Offices were located. I stepped off the elevator on the 11th floor and went into Lewis' office.

I looked at my wristwatch and it was 9:55am. I opened the door and walked to the glass window and announced myself to the receptionist.

She smiled warmly and said, "Mr. Avrech, Mr. Lewis will be right with you."

My heart skipped a beat. It was finally time. I couldn't wait to hear what he would say. I was all ears.

Lewis opened the door and there stood a man about six feet tall, white wavy hair, glasses and a white mustache. With a big smile on his face, he reached his outstretched hand to me and with a firm handshake said, "Nice to finally meet you Larry, I'm Dick."

I shook his hand and felt like I had just met God.

CHAPTER FIFTEEN

SUCCESS IS THE BEST
REVENGE/FAMOUS CASES WORKED

IN MAY OF 1987, I filled out an application to become a Private Investigator. The requirement in California was to accumulate 6000 hours of investigative experience verified.

I sought the help of one of my "Life Savers," Lieutenant John Morrison. He was an investigative Lieutenant at Northeastern Division and was more than happy to verify my hours for the State of California.

I took the exam in Los Angeles a few months later and successfully passed. I was doing more difficult services requiring skip tracing which require a license to perform.

One day in February of 1988, I was at the courthouse doing research when I ran into Bob Edgett. Bob worked as a Traffic Investigator while on the department. He was no longer with the department and was now a Private Investigator with his own company, American Professional Investigations. I told Bob I was looking for work.

Edgett said, "I really don't have time to research these cases for the Attorneys. Would you be interested in doing it for me?"

I jumped at the chance and the rest is history.

After numerous jobs, terminations and disappointments, I swore if I didn't follow through with my vow to get my badge back, I would still be a success. Success is the best revenge.

I thought this could possibly work into something big. Bob was now doing accident reconstruction work keeping him plenty busy locally and abroad. Bob gave me a list and told me to check for products liability, negligence and wrongful death cases every month and send him the list of cases with an invoice.

Edgett liked my work and spoke to Bob Townsend, an in-house investigator for Gage, Mazursky, Schwartz, Angelo and Kussman, a heavy hitting Beverly Hills law firm. The firm only handled six and seven figure cases. I would handle and help them win many famous cases.

DARRELL MILLS CASE

In August of 1987, I received a phone call from San Diego attorney, Richard (Dick) Trost. He was defending a client, Darrell Mills against a charge of Battery on a minor child.

Mills owned a business that leased laser printers. His client was behind in the amount of $300.00 and it was arranged for him to come and pick up the item. Mills came with an employee on February 17, 1987 to assist Mills in picking up the printer. They approached the house and went to a sliding glass door. After announcing their presence, the 14-year-old daughter of the client opened the door.

The printer was in plain view and they told her arrangements were made to pick up the item.

The daughter refused them entrance stating no one was home, even though her uncle was watching on a closed-circuit television from another room.

They were tired of excuses and walked past her into the residence to pick up the item. The Uncle entered the room and told them to leave. They left without the item and drove a short distance away to contact the Sheriff's Department. They were advised this was a civil matter and they could not intervene.

A short time later the father returned and was told Mills had side stepped his daughter and forcibly entered and as a result twisted her left hand. She lost her balance and fell against a wooden desk, injuring her back. The father demanded prosecution. The Sheriff's Detective Dodd after doing a follow-up investigation requested the District Attorney file charges against Mills for Battery on a Juvenile.

After receiving the information on the case,* I began interviewing witnesses. I confirmed an employee of Mills spoke to the client and was told he could come in the evening after five and pick up his printer.

A former independent contractor was interviewed. He worked with both parties and was present the night of the incident. The lessee asked him to come over and disconnect the printer. When he arrived, several hours after the incident, he saw the alleged, injured daughter, "skipping around" in the house. Her father (lessee) didn't feel she was hurt and this witness suggested he take her to a doctor. When the witness was in business with Mills he was bought out. The lessee thought there was some bitterness on the witnesses' part against Mills and felt he could talk freely to him.

The witness was at the lessee's house on numerous occasions when creditors would call and he'd tell them he had no money to pay. The witness made the statement to me that (Gus) the lessee would say anything to get out from having to pay someone to whom he owed money.

Mill's employee, Cole stated when interviewed he stood right behind

Mills and at no time did he put his hands on or cause the alleged victim to lose her balance and fall.

On August 6, 1987 I telephoned the Offices of Dr. William Greenway and spoke with his receptionist. I informed her I was a private investigator looking into the Trista Janis case. I explained I already obtained a copy of her medical history, dated February 19, 1987, two days after the alleged incident. I asked her if this was Trista's first visit?

The receptionist checked the file and indicated it was her first and only visit and she didn't return for any follow-up visits.

On October 6, 1987 I drove to Vista High School to interview the alleged victim. I spoke with the Assistant Principal.

She asked me what my purpose was, and did I obtain the parent's permission.

I explained to her that was my original intention, but I was unable to do so. I provided her with the home phone number.

The Assistant Principal spoke with an adult woman named Lisa who understood my purpose and knew I was working for Mr. Mills.

Lisa told the Assistant Principal, "Oh okay." She thought the school was calling about her being tardy. When she fully understood the purpose, she gave her permission for me to talk to Trista. Currently Trista was in between classes and a monitor was sent to bring her to the office.

Once there, I was joined by Dr. Dan Grider, Trista's Principal. He asked if he could be in attendance during the interview.

I told him absolutely. Then, I explained to Trista I needed to interview her regarding the incident, and I would take her recorded statement.

Trista objected saying she didn't want to record it unless her father knew.

I asked her questions without using the tape recorder. My first question to her was, "Where were you injured?"

Trista answered by placing her right hand across her body, even though her left hand was the supposed injured hand and, her left hand was closest to me.

I said, "So he injured your right hand?"

Trista answered, "Yes my right hand."

I asked her, "If you were injured, why didn't you go to the hospital?"

Trista said, "I don't like hospitals, they scare me."

My next question was, "Did you go to the doctor the next day?"

She replied, "Yes."

I asked, "Was that Dr. Greenway?"

Trista said, "Yes."

"How long have you been going to Dr. Greenway?" I asked.

Trista said, "A long time, as long as I can remember."

I inquired, "This wasn't the first visit you ever made?"

Trista added, "No, he's my family doctor. I've been going to Dr. Greenway..." then she paused and asked looked at the Principal and asked him, "How long have I been going here, since 1985?" Then she looked back at me and said, "I've been going to Dr. Greenway since 1985."

I asked, "Where was your uncle during this incident?"

Trista replies, "In the shower."

I probed, "So, you lied when you told Mr. Mills that nobody else was home?"

Trista said, "Well my uncle was in the shower and wouldn't have been able to help me."

As a result of this interview, I caught Trista in four lies. The first lie was regarding which hand was injured.

A bench trial was set for October 13, 1987 but was continued to November 30, 1987.

On November 24, 1987 I wrote and served a Subpoena Duces Tecum for production of evidence along with a subpoena for the custodian of records for the Offices of Dr. William Greenway.

I wrote my subpoena's like I wrote out search warrants. I left nothing to chance when requesting evidence.

A bench trial was held on November 30, 1987. After Trista testified to the incident I was put on the stand and testified. The custodian of records was called and testified to the fact Trista only visited the Dr. Greenway once and never returned. She also testified her left hand was treated and not the right hand, as she conveyed to me.

When you lie you must recall what you said. Trista was caught in a web of lies and the Judge had no alternative but to find Darrell Mills not guilty.

BRANDENBURG A-4 SKYHAWK CRASH

On October 21, 1987 I received a call from Attorney Ray Johnson, from Gage, Mazursky, Schwartz, Angelo and Kussman. Johnson briefed me on a Products Liability/Wrongful Death case involving a Navy Pilot, Lieutenant Commander Steven Lee Brandenburg who was killed when his A-4 Skyhawk went into an inverted roll and crashed on his final approach to National Guard Airbase, Buckley

Field, in Aurora, Colorado. The date of the crash was October 22, 1984.

Brandenburg attempted to eject from the plane, however the aircraft was out of a safe ejection envelope. His plane impacted the ground approximately 1.5-miles from the approach end of runway 32.

A problem existed with the leading-edge slats on the plane and it was necessary to locate a California Defendant either a supplier or a manufacturer/vendor of the slat and roller bearing track system and serve them before the end of the month.

Later that day, I went to Fighter Town, "Top Gun" at Miramar Naval Airbase and contacted Lieutenant Commander Roger Daddiomoff, a pilot who flew in the same squad as the deceased.

Daddiomoff stated there are three tracks on each wing operated by either high angles, known as angles of attack or at low speed. The pilot could delay the operation of the slats by pushing back on the control. Normal operation would cause the slat to move forward on their roller bearings and drop into place. Due to icing on the wings, one slat deployed farther than the other causing the plane to roll.

Since the crash in October of 1984 there was another crash in Nevada in the summer of 1987 where the slats failed to operate properly. The pilot, Pat Paris was able to eject safely.

On October 22, 1987, I drove to the San Diego Aerospace Museum and researched books on the plane. The museum has an A-4B Skyhawk in the Exhibit Hall. I took pictures but the lighting was poor and they didn't develop well. I subsequently made two additional trips to obtain the necessary shots. I also found two books on the A-4, one written by the engineer who built the A-4, Ed Heinemann.

The following day, I made some newspaper inquiries regarding the crash to see if I could locate any articles. I also went to libraries and two major bookstores to research data on the A-4.

On June 27, 1987, I sought information regarding where I could locate Ed Heinemann. I contacted the people at the Registrar of Voters office in San Diego and discovered Heinemann was living in the City of Rancho Santa Fe and got his phone number.

Later the same morning, I contacted Ed Heinemann at home and told him I had a friend who was interested in jet fighter planes and was specifically interested in the A-4. I asked if he could explain the slat system to me.

Heinemann said the inventor of the slat system was a man named Hadley Paige, in Great Britain. Heinemann said when he put slats on the A-4, Paige couldn't believe Heinemann would put such a system on such a thin wing. Paige sent an engineer from England, a Dr. Lachmann to California to observe the fact Heinemann put a slat system into a plane which was normally used on thicker wings. Heinemann said if I was really interested in more of his development of the A-4, I should purchase one of his books and I could come to his house where he had several models of the A-4.

I asked Heinemann if a person wanted to build a replica of the A-4 where would they go to obtain the necessary materials necessary to make the slats.

Heinemann said, "A project of that magnitude would be very costly. Some people previously contacted him to do such a project. They ran out of money and abandoned it."

I asked Heinemann, "If money were no object where would I go?"

Heinemann said. "There wouldn't be anyone in California who would do the work unless you went to McDonnell-Douglas and asked them to build it for you." Heinemann gave me the name of Harry Gann, the Historian at McDonnell-Douglas in Long Beach.

Later in the day I drove back to the San Diego Aerospace Museum and with the assistance of the Museum staff, I used a ladder, worked the slat system and took closer shots. It should be noted; no improvements of the slat system were made on the A-4A and A4-S models.

I found a book titled, "The Great Book of Modern War Airplanes" *published by Portland House. It describes the McDonnell-Douglas F-4 Phantom as the plane that replaced the A-4 Skyhawk. It also mentioned the slats for the Phantom were produced by the Beech Aircraft Company in Kansas.

The next day, I called the Beech Aircraft Company in Wichita, Kansas and asked if they did any work on the A-4 as well? On October 29, 1987 I received a call from Pat Zerbe, Human Relations spokesperson for Beech Aircraft. She indicated they didn't work on the A-4.

A lawsuit was filed against McDonnell Douglas and served in a timely fashion

BOB CROWE EXTORTION CASE

In March of 1988, I was President of the San Diego Chapter of the T.I.P.S. Club. It was a business referral club that met every Monday morning at the campus of National University in Mission Valley. Our group included Attorneys, Plumbing Contractors, Builders, Printers, Insurance Brokers and a host of other small business owners. Before we started our meeting, Bob Crowe from Flagmasters, a flag and banner business in Chula Vista, approached me and mentioned he needed to speak with me after the meeting.

When the meeting concluded, Crowe cornered me and said his truck was left downtown last week when he met with friends for dinner. When he returned to his vehicle, it was broken into and his briefcase was stolen. Inside the briefcase were airline tickets and his Income Tax information.

Crowe reported the theft, but since then he was receiving phone calls supposedly from a friend of the person responsible for the theft. He was told to meet the man downtown that evening. It would cost him $500.00 to get his property back. Quickly, the price went up to $1,000.00 and Crow didn't know what to do. The extortionist was supposed to call back later in the day and firm up the arrangements.

I told Crowe to agree to any arrangement he made and agree to anything. Then wait to hear from me, I needed to make a phone call. I called John Morrison, my Lieutenant friend and asked, "Who's the Central Division Investigative Lieutenant?"

He said, "Ron Seden."

I said, "Great!" Seden was the Lieutenant who took my badge away back in 1985. I thought to myself he'd never work with me

John said, "Don't worry, I'll handle it."

Morrison called Seden and said, "Ron, I have an extortion going down in your area tonight. How many men can you spare me?"

Seden said, "How about a Sergeant, two detectives and two patrolmen."

In the meantime, Crowe called me back with the arrangements and I briefed Morrison.

Morrison said, "Make sure your friend doesn't mention your name to any of the officers he talks to."

Crowe went to the arranged location with officers in place, waiting. The suspect appeared and walked towards Crowe carrying his brief-case. He asked Crowe to identify himself.

Crowe did so.

Then the suspect asked Crowe if he brought the money?

Crowe responded, "Yes I did."

With split second timing the officers sprang into action and took the suspect down. The suspect was packing an ice pick and a knife.

Crowe stood the possibility of being robbed and stabbed. The suspect had no intention of returning Crowe's briefcase and every intention of making Crowe a fatal statistic.

Until now, Seden never knew I was behind the scenes. If not for my "Life Saver," John Morrison, Crowe would most assuredly have been injured or killed.

Better check your desk Lieutenant Seden, I may have borrowed back my badge for the evening. You can take the badge from the cop, but you can't take the cop from the badge.

HEATHER O'ROURKE (POLTERGEIST) CHILD STAR WRONGFUL DEATH

On May 25, 1988 I received a packet in the mail from the Beverly Hills Law Offices of Sanford Gage. It contained instructions on the filing of a wrongful death suit for Heather O'Rourke, a child star discovered by Steven Spielberg who starred in Poltergeist, Poltergeist II and Poltergeist III. It was filed on behalf of her mother who was the Administrator of her daughter's estate. The suit claimed Heather was misdiagnosed by Kaiser doctors first for flu-like symptoms, then an inflammation of her bowel caused by a parasite (Guardia) which was found to be in the well water in Big Bear, California where Heather lived. The problem was a congenital intestinal blockage, (stenosis). It should've been diagnosed by Doctors at Kaiser but was instead treated as Crohn's disease with steroids. A simple surgical procedure removing the area of intestine that was narrowed and resected the two ends together would have brought her back to health again.

On January 31, 1988, Heather woke up vomiting. While waiting for paramedics to show up, she collapsed. She was taken to Kaiser Hospital where she went into cardiac arrest and then taken to Children's Hospital where her pupils were fixed. Children's Hospital did everything possible to save her, but it was too late. She was pronounced dead at 2:43 pm February 1, 1988.

Heather wanted to direct films when she was older and could read 60 pages of script an hour memorizing her lines as well as other cast members' lines. Her last words were spoken to her mother. She said, "I love you."

After filing the lawsuit in San Diego Superior Court on Wednesday May 25, 1988, I was tasked with going up to the Big Bear area to check local dumps in the area for bacteria and take water samples to check for the Guardia parasite. This wasn't to confirm, but to eliminate the possibility.

An economist was hired to figure out her net worth should she have survived, which was figured at over ten million dollars.

Heather was born in San Diego on December 27, 1975 and was just 12 years old at the time of her death. She was signed the day after Steven Spielberg offered her the part. Drew Barrymore was also up for the part. She was known for her two famous lines, "They're here!" and "They're baa-aack!"

JERRY CROSS LOCATE FOR THE F.B.I.

In December of 1989, I received a call from Kevin Tracy, an immigration attorney, who worked in a firm with Bob Schroth and Jerry Cross. Cross had his name on the marquee and on stationary he was listed as, "of counsel." He was an immigration attorney and passed the Indiana Bar. But he wasn't currently practicing in San Diego. He was more interested in swindling people out of their money from a gold futures scam.

Cross was under investigation by the F.B.I. for the scam as his investors were in contact with the F.B.I. The bureau didn't know Jerry's current whereabouts to put their hands on him.

Cross seemed to just drop out of sight. Since Schroth and Tracy shared office space with Cross, his victims thought Tracy and Schroth were involved in the scam and were named in the action.

Tracy and others asked me to locate and serve Jerry Cross. After doing some research I located a brother of Jerry's living in Moline, Illinois, the home of John Deere tractor company.

I obtained a phone number and called the house. A man answered the phone. I said, "Is this the Steve Cross residence?"

He said, "No, this is the Jerry Cross residence."

I said, "You didn't happen to go to Calumet High School, did you?"

He said, "No, I'm from California sorry."

Armed with several Summons and Complaints from his victims and a round trip ticket to Chicago, I flew to O'Hare and was met by my Dad. He drove me out to his McHenry Firestone Store he owned and arranged a rental car for me to drive the 158-mile trip to Moline.

Once I arrived, I sat down the street from the house and watched it for about twenty minutes. Then, I noticed Jerry come out to shovel the snow from his driveway. I approached him and said, "Hey Jerry!" and served him all the Summons and Complaints I brought.

I left immediately, went to the nearest phone to call the local branch of the F.B.I. and told them where they could find Jerry Cross.

It was a 178-mile drive back to my folk's condo in Northbrook, Illinois. I spent the weekend with them before returning to California. It was good to see my parents. My trip there was totally unexpected and my Mom was in poor health. My short visit perked her right up.

DAVID VOGEL HATE CRIME CASE

David Vogel was a Polish Jew with a heavy European accent, being tormented at his National City Pawnbrokers business and his home by phone callers.

They sought to injure, oppress, threaten and intimidate a Jewish citizen of the United States who was an inhabitant of California.

They would say, "This is Adolf Hitler calling, this is Joseph Mengele calling, do you have any Jews for sale, any Niggers for sale. You should have died in Treblinka and we're going to keep calling until we hear you have a heart attack on the other end of the phone line."

Later they threatened to do him bodily harm and finally they threatened to kill him.

This went on unabated for several years. They'd call his business sometimes as many as a dozen times a day. Vogel didn't know what to do. It all started back in 1987.

Vogel's family was exterminated in the concentration camps during World War II and he and his wife were reliving the war all over again live through the terror every day. He lost two cousins and his aunt and uncle in the camps. Vogel was lucky to be alive as he fled Nazi Germany in 1938 when he was a teenager.

Up until 1989, the F.B.I. characterized this as discrimination or harassment. There were no Hate Crime violation statutes until 1990.

Vogel would report the calls to the National City Police Department and they told him to either change his phone number or move. He also inquired of the F.B.I. and was told they couldn't do anything for him.

In March of 1990, I was doing service work and investigations for my Attorney, Donald S. Peterson. He did his best to represent me with my investigation on the police department, but he was working against a stacked deck. Anthony (Tony) Caputo was also an attorney I worked for on cases. There was a third attorney in the office, Phillip Altfest who did mostly Probate work. While there, Altfest told me Vogel worshipped at the same Temple and he confided in Altfest what he was experiencing almost daily for the last few years. Altfest told Vogel he may know of someone who could help.

Altfest gave me Vogel's information and I spoke to him and got a history of events. I told Vogel I'd make some calls and get back to him.

I knew Tony Di Lorenzo from the Bureau. He worked the bank robbery detail and I usually saw him three to four times a month back when bank robberies were a common event. I called him and asked if he knew anyone in the Civil Rights Division I could talk to.

Tony said, "Yeah me, I just got transferred"

I told him what Vogel was experiencing.

Tony said, "I love it, let's run with it."

The same day the bureau met with Vogel at his business to hook up recording equipment on his phone. While the F.B.I. agents were still present the first of over 100 calls came in. The timing couldn't have been better.

Additionally, the callers put Vogel's name in a gay newspaper. So, in addition to the terrorizing calls he also started receiving calls from homosexual men who wanted to meet Vogel in the desert for trysts.

During the bureau's investigation, it was also uncovered the suspects were using unauthorized long-distance telephone access codes as well as related phone numbers to make long distance calls and send material on their computers.

Most of the calls made to Vogel were from a pay phone in the South Bay area of San Diego. The callers were identified and five suspects including three adults and two juveniles* were arrested on a six-count indictment presented to a Federal Grand Jury.

This case was the first conviction for a hate crime in San Diego for the offices of the F.B.I. under Gary Laturno.

BOSTON RAPE CASE

On June 28, 1991 I received a call from Attorney Maynard Kartvedt. I provided services and conducted investigations for him. His office was across the street from mine in El Cajon.

Kartvedt stated he had a colleague friend who went to law school with him, now practicing in the Boston, Massachusetts area. He was representing a client who was charged with raping his secretary.

Neither the attorney, nor his client knew much about the alleged victim, except she was from California. He asked Kartvedt if he knew any investigators who could do some background checks on the secretary.

The client told Staples he owned a business and he just hired a secretary. The client's vehicle was in for repairs and his secretary was driving him everywhere to make his meetings. The client's car was repaired and in appreciation for her driving him around to make his meetings, he offered to take her out for dinner. She accepted his invitation and they went out.

The client was a married man. One thing lead to another and they wound up at a motel for consensual sex. His mistake.

Everything went south. The secretary knew he was married and saw dollar signs. Although they had consensual sex; she threw down the rape card.

His client was arrested and facing a trial.

Kartvedt gave me Staples phone number and I called him. Staples gave me the information he had off her job application and I told him, I'd get back to him.

I called a friend on the department and asked him to check this person out. He got back with me and said she had a Bench Warrant in NCIC (National Crime Information Center) charging an FTA (Failure to Appear) on a theft case out of the San Jose, Police Department.

I got the warrant information which was San Jose's case number and called my brother who lived in San Jose. I told him to copy everything in the file, get it certified and send it Federal Express to me overnight.

The following day, I received the information from my brother, made copies and forwarded it to Staples.

Apparently, on August 4, 1986, when employed at the San Jose Macy's store, "things were slow." The employee decided to steal some clothing and conceal it in shopping bags which she put by the customer service department. At the end of her shift, she carried the bags out the employee exit and was stopped by security. The price tags were still on the items and she couldn't provide receipts. She was placed under arrest for Petty Theft, shoplifting.

She was given a court date of October 6, 1986. The suspect failed to appear and fled the jurisdiction of the court. A bench warrant was issued the same day and was placed in the N.C.I.C. system.

Staples was in court in trial on this case when two Marshal's entered the courtroom and placed the alleged victim under arrest. The suspect, Goldsmith moved several times before arriving in Mass-achusetts.

When faced with the apparent trouble she was now in, she admitted in court she fabricated the rape story. The charges against Staples client were dropped.

I never once left my office and never spoke to Staples client; but I saved him from having to face a rape trial from 3,000 miles away and justice was served.

LOCATED FATHER AFTER 28 YEARS

On a cold wintry December 16, 1999, I was in my warm, comfortable office when a woman in her late twenties walked in.

She told me she was born and raised in Alabama by her mother after she divorced her husband. The young woman was just two years old at the time of the divorce. She was now just turning 30 and had twin sons, six years old. One was in desperate need of heart surgery. She was a single mother on A.F.D.C (Aid to Families with Dependent Children) and wanted to know how much it would cost to locate her father.

I invited her to sit down and tell me her story. She supplied me with all the information she could.

She provided her father's name, date of birth and place of birth. Her mother had since passed away and no other relative or further information was available.

I told her I charged for the attempt, not the results and I made no guarantees.

She told me others tried and were unsuccessful and she felt they just took her money.

I told her it would cost her a flat $300.00.

Could she make payments? she asked me.

I said, "Of course."

She began to pull out a wad of money, all singles. "How much do you need?"

I told her, "One dollar."

She said, "That's it?"

I said, "For now."

I told her to go home and I would call her.

I checked data banks first to see if he died. There was no record. I found a person living in Valley Center, California out in the North County of San Diego, east of Escondido. He had the same name, date of birth and he was born in Alabama. All I needed now was a phone contact number. It was an unlisted number.

I knew someone at San Diego Gas and Electric who gave me the fathers phone number from the address.

When doing locates, I never gave the information to my client, until I contacted the other party and told them someone was looking for them. Would it be permissible to give them your phone number?

I called and spoke to the client's father, explained to him his daughter hired me to locate him. I explained her circumstances for trying to find him and her failed efforts. She desperately needed to reconnect with her father.

He started to cry and said he attempted for many years to find his daughter but was looking for her in Alabama. He enthusiastically gave me permission for her to call him.

It was only 30 minutes since the young woman left my office. I reached her by phone and told her I found her father.

She burst into tears and said, "You're lying to me. You couldn't have found him so fast."

I told her, "I just got off the phone with him. Would you like his phone number?"

She composed herself and took down the number. She said, "I'll call you back, when I finish talking to him."

The client called me back about an hour later to tell me she spent half the time crying on the phone with her father. She told me he was a wealthy farmer who re-married and he invited her family up to his house for Christmas, where she'd be part of his family. She thanked me so much for my help and wanted to know when she needed to pay?

I asked if she could come back to the office?

She said, "I'll be right down."

An hour later she came through the door to tell me her father called her back and said he was willing to give her an open check for her son's heart surgery. And, would she consider moving up with his family. She was so excited and thanked me again.

I told her as a Christmas present, I wouldn't charge her and gave her the dollar back.

About ten days later, I received a call from her. Her father bought her a new car for Christmas and she was moving her family up to Valley Center to live with him and her new Stepmom.

PART TWO

CHAPTER SIXTEEN

WORKING WITH DICK BEFORE THE TASK FORCE

In Chapter 14, I described my original meeting with Deputy District Attorney Richard "Dick" J. Lewis as meeting God. In our first meeting, after all the initial pleasantries, we talked and learned about each other. Dick collected Die cast cars and I collected Comic Books. We were both married with children and dog lovers

Here was a man who followed my case and knew I was set up by my department and said he could prove it.

Why did I call him a God? Simple. He was a higher authority than what I was used to dealing with in the Department. As a prosecutor, he would have the final say over matters to be prosecuted.

A real plus for Dick was his background in Law Enforcement. He came up through the ranks as a Detective Lieutenant in Homicide and Criminal Intelligence. He explained the system the Police Department used regarding the funds which they paid to informants. This fund couldn't be audited by the city.

He knew about Gentile's one-time handler, Detective Larry Lindstrom. Apparently, the department went to great lengths to keep

Gentile's prior informant status a secret from me, the troops and the press. Prior to meeting Dick, I could only allege she was an informant. It wasn't until later I had confirmation it was true. Internal Affairs referred to her as a "spirited citizen" when they knew full well, she was an informant.

Let me break down the role of an informant. They aren't on the payroll. They don't sit around like an out of work carpenter at a union hall waiting for the next job. Either the person would contact a department with information, or, the department contacted a person with questions. The department would decide whether the information was credible or not. If it was worth pursuing and, whether the informant was completely reliable or not. If he or she was reliable, she'd be assigned a code name or number. Informants weren't always paid money. I'll use the word "compensated." If their information paid off, they might be compensated monetarily, or, they might have pending cases against them dismissed with approval from a high-ranking member of the department and/or with the cooperation of the District Attorney's Office or the City Attorney's Office. If this happened it was often reflected on their rap sheet as, "Dismissed in the Interests of Justice." Or in the "furtherance of justice." If you were an established informant, you might be contacted by your handler and asked to assist in an assignment. One of the requirements was an informant with a criminal history shouldn't be out committing crimes.

Gentile was an active prostitute and was trying to work both sides of the fence. The department knew this. She was the biggest single problem on the streets. When the other girls left the streets or travel to another city, Gentile was still on the streets plying her trade.

So, let's extinguish the myth a police informant is a full time, get rich quick arrangement. It is neither full-time nor get rich quick. Informants don't receive a stipend as some people think.

The Prostitution Enforcement Detail was formed based on the model program used in San Jose, California, which was highly effective.

Prostitution in San Diego was out of control in the early 1980's, along with the crimes associated with it. Gentile was a large part of the problem.

While prostitutes don't like being busted for attempting to make a living from the sex trade, most would try and "chummy up" to officers with the intent of gaining some type of reciprocal help when they needed a favor. I had one such individual on the street, but it wasn't Gentile. When she was arrested, she called several officers at Eastern looking to help her, but we were unable to do so.

When I was under investigation, my Sergeant Harold Goudarzi, contacted her looking to find some dirt on me and was surprised to hear her response. "Oh no, he's all business. I lied to him once and he said, if I ever lied to him again, he'd put me in jail. He stops me, gets his information and I tell him the truth."

The ladies of the evening knew, even though we were on opposite sides of the law, if they needed help, we were out there for them as well.

In the early days putting together my case, I met with Dick almost every morning through the noon hour. I brought my case paperwork to him and we discussed it at length while his staff was processing my documents and number stamping my pages.

We went over the Department's investigation. What the department thought was evidence against me, were the tape-recorded phone conversations between Gentile and myself.

Dick thought they were comical. He said, "How the hell were you supposed to talk with her? You used vulgarity, told dirty jokes and made insinuations, because she was a street person. That's the language they hear and best understand. I can understand just from the subject matter you were trying to keep her on the line and get her in a talking mood. You were trying to reel her in and extract information."

Dick thought I stood a good chance of being reinstated and encouraged me to try.

But I had stepped on too many toes and once reinstated, the department could fire me for wearing a black sock and a brown sock. They wouldn't need a reason a second time.

Dick agreed.

He would comment to me, "Boy they sure didn't like your "Snow White" appearance. You fought for what was right and wouldn't turn your back on anything occurring."

Lewis, in retrospect said, "You should've done things differently, but you were a young officer who found himself up against insurmountable odds." According to Lewis, Black should've been fired period. His past record showed, he should've been removed years earlier.

Until I met Dick Lewis, I never thought I had a ghost of a chance in hell of ever straightening out the Gentile case and clearing my name.

So much has occurred since meeting with Dick and I learned and grew from the experience. I'll never be able to repay him for what he did for me. He changed my life, gave me hope, cleared my name and followed through on every promise he made. I owe a great deal to this man.

During the seven years I collaborated with Dick on Task Force cases, we only took a few months hiatus when he had hip replacement surgery. During the time he was off recuperating, I remained in constant communication with him.

By the end of 1986, there were approximately 20 bodies found dumped in the county.*

Twenty-one if you counted Carol De Felice who was murdered February 24, 1984. This was 22 bodies too many. But the model the Task Force adopted when they formed in 1988 was only women who were murdered from January 1985 forward. Otherwise, De Felice would've been a Task Force case.

I told Dick, the murders had nothing to do with the women's lifestyle or the chances they took. Nevertheless, no one deserved to die as these women did.

We discussed the Daniel Stafford case and Dick asked if I thought Stafford would be able to travel by car from San Diego to Seattle in between assaults. The Task Force was checking out the possibility of whether the San Diego suspects were also connected to any of the Green River cases long before the media made the suggestion there might be a connection.

The topic of those victims whose necks were broken in the same fashion as Donna's neck was broken was raised.

I thought to myself and said, "Either a Wrestler/Bouncer type, a Martial Arts person or a trained (Armed Forces) Killing Machine would be capable of doing those things."

Dick said, "Do you know if Carl Black was a wrestler in high school?"

I said, "I haven't the slightest idea. It's not like I shared locker space with him. I respected his rank, but personally I never cared for the man." But it was something to consider.

Dick and I discussed the formation of the Homicide Task Force and was told retired Deputy District Attorney Charles (Chuck) Rogers was coming out of retirement to head the unit for District Attorney Ed Miller. I met with Rogers who assured me he wasn't through with Carl Black. Not by a long shot.

The District Attorney's Office knew other information about the San Diego Police Department. I was told Kolender must've been extremely paranoid about being investigated as their office knew Kolender regularly swept his office for listening devices.

When Ronald Elliot Porter was arrested for the attempted murder of Annette Russell in October of 1988, I recognized his face from a 7-Eleven® store at 5202 El Cajon Boulevard.*

Further checking revealed, Porter applied to register to vote with the Registrar of Voters Office and gave an address of 4346 52nd Street #6.* Less than a half a block away and within walking distance from the 7-Eleven® store. The date on the document was May 7, 1984 which would put him in the area of where the prostitutes worked and were last reported missing.

I turned this information over to Dick in January of 1989 and subsequently gave it to Task Force detectives Dave Ayers and Gary Murphy at my attorney's office, January 14, 1989.

In 1989, nothing was done on the Gentile case. No one was sharing information and, if someone's theory didn't coincide with another investigator's version it was dismissed.

Dick told me a story which gave me a déjà vu moment. When Dick first came to the District Attorney's office having run the Criminal Intelligence unit with the Sheriff's department in San Bernardino, he wanted to start a third Intelligence agency within the DA's office as well.

Deputy Chief Ken O'Brien thought two agencies were quite enough and vehemently opposed the move to the point where he tried to set up Dick with a hooker who supposedly had information for him about a case. O'Brien, hoped to catch Dick in a compromising situation, where he'd be arrested, fired and humiliated. This is the extent O'Brien would go to have his way.

But Dick saw through O'Brien's scheme and it never came to fruition.

I thought, wait a minute. A high-ranking officer on the department used a hooker to try and entrap someone to get him fired. It's like déjà vu, where have I heard that before?

Dick asked me if I kept any of my information on the girls I contacted on the street?

I told him I kept all my Journals and all my Field Interrogation slips which would denote scars and tattoos to help him identify bodies if it became necessary.

We worked on my paperwork and I was helped with the necessary points to cover in my lawsuit against Chief William Kolender and the City of San Diego.* After the filing of my right to sue letter* which is a joke in itself. All it provides is stalling time for the city. They are supposed to respond within 45 days of receipt of the form. The 45 days expired, and I didn't hear anything. I guess they figure in the 45 days witnesses might die, change their mind, maybe you couldn't afford an attorney or find no attorney would take the case as I did, or maybe I'd die in the meantime. Finally, I received the denial letter from the city telling me I'd have to seek action through the courts.

I started attorney shopping and was told, "I need $50,000 up front to start with, then more as we go with no guarantee." Or, "I'm a close personal friend of Police Chief Bill Kolender and would never oppose him." Or, "I'd be afraid to file an action against him." Others said it would be an arduous, lengthy process and would tie up their other cases or, they were too busy. I checked larger firms in Los Angeles and got the same answers. There wasn't a firm in San Diego or Los Angeles able to take my case. At the time, I was barely making it financially so I couldn't afford the attorneys I spoke to who wanted large fees in advance, and no one would take my case on a contingency basis.

In the meantime, the city was paper working me to death and requesting I submit paperwork to them or incur monetary court sanctions. I was unable to provide the city with the requested paperwork and was forced to drop my lawsuit against the city. Without an experienced attorney, a city entity can paperwork you to death.*

WORKING WITH DICK DURING THE TASK FORCE

While 1990 was a pretty good year for me with Dick later taking over as Head of the Homicide Task Force, another group of Serial Killings were occurring in San Diego proper. Cleophus Prince was committing burglaries all over San Diego and murdered six women. He was known as the Clairemont Killer, despite the fact he murdered a single victim in East San Diego and a mother and daughter in University City. One of the victim's was raped and all were stabbed to death multiple times. Law Enforcement resources were stretched thin investigating two serial killing series' simultaneously.

It was fall of 1990, Dick was now in the driver's seat of the Task Force. There was no more crap going on. Bonnie Dumanis was now a Juvenile Referee and Goudarzi was no longer a member of the Task Force.

My education with Dick started out small. He used blank calendar forms to track his cases day by day.* Next, I was taught how to write Subpoena Duces Tecum's to produce evidence.

He said, "Write them with the same language you'd use in a Search Warrant."

I listened and I learned. Later, I put these skills to use when working my own PI cases. I was able to request information most attorneys would either forget or, have no knowledge of the existence of such information or, how to go about requesting it.

I continued my Investigation business and wrote all my subpoena duces tecums and affidavits on all cases requiring the production of evidence and specialized in obtaining tapes from law enforcement agencies which helped win cases for attorneys who used my services.

One day at breakfast, I asked Dick, "What if I need information in a case requiring the exhumation of a body? Not expecting it would ever come up, but if it did."

A few days later, he provided me with a case from the DA's office. It contained notes in his handwriting with the proper language to use, along with the motions and autopsy report.*

Even though I considered writing a book about all this someday, Dick would say, "Tiger, one day you'll write a book about all this stuff." However, I wasn't completely and officially cleared for years.

After passing my initial polygraph in 1986, I swore I'd never put myself under so much stress. Sure, I knew I wasn't guilty of anything, but it was still a stressful experience. However, I broke the promise I made myself, when Dick asked if I'd take a test by the Police Department's expert, Paul Redden. It wasn't a question of believing me, but the first polygraph I took and passed was from Dick's friend and former partner Don Hardy. So, to show everything was on the up and up, I took a second test.

Arrangements were made to come to a hotel room at the old Howard Johnson's off Waring Road. Sheriff's Sergeant Jim Cooke was with the Task Force at the time, accompanied by Redden, * I was apprehensive, but this needed to be done. The first time I was nervous, but I was in friendly surroundings with Hardy. This time was different because I wasn't in friendly surroundings. Once again, I passed with flying colors. Now, no one could come back and question my credibility or anything. This time, I passed with the Police Department's expert. It was another step toward completely exonerating myself.

Some of my discussions with Dick were not police related. I recall a conversation about one of his sons' having problems. I don't recall if it was John or Richard, but as a father, I gave him some advice.

Much time was wasted running down unsubstantiated rumors of Donna Gentile being on a tape with former Sheriff John Duffy and

Bill Kolender. Detectives in 1990 sifted through 750 tapes in the possession of Thomas Irwin, better known as D.J. "Shotgun Tom Kelly."

Additionally, time was spent going to the Philippines to return Rolodex Madam Karen Wilkening, to check out the possibility of a connection between Wilkening and Donna Gentile. Also, whether Carl Black and Robert Hannibal plotted the death of Donna Gentile in a room at the Hitching Post Motel. All these turned out to be dead-end claims which required a great amount of Investigative time. Still, they needed to be focused upon and eliminated from consideration.

In May of 1992, Sheriff Jim Roache inherited problems of his own with a backlog of 175 Homicides to investigate and pulled his detectives out prior to the Task Force disbanding.

During the mid-eighties, just one or two counties away, another group of serial killings of prostitutes were occurring in Riverside and San Bernardino.

Choked, stabbed and dumped. This series of murders were later solved by a joint Task Force comprised of officers from the Riverside County and San Bernardino departments.

Dick wasn't only checking similarities with the Green River Task Force, but closer to home as well. The killings would be solved in 1992 with the arrest of William Lester Suff. He was well-named the Lake Elsinore Killer and /or the Riverside Prostitute Killer.

Let's face it, name a large metropolitan city in the United States and you will find serial killings of prostitutes. Murder claims no boundaries.

CHAPTER SEVENTEEN

TASK FORCE CASES

BETWEEN 1985 AND 1993 bodies were dropping in San Diego County like flies. The citizens of San Diego didn't know what to think. Was the Green River Killer paying them a visit? Were the two killing series' related?

During my time working with Dick Lewis, I followed the other killings as well as the Gentile case and was informed from time to time. But you must understand, my primary focus was clearing my name by helping solve the Gentile homicide.

There are gaps with my overall information on some victims and their murders. However, if I inquired regarding any other case, I would've been brought up to speed on anything.

I was given assignments by Lewis which to this day, I won't discuss.

In this chapter, I'll attempt to humanize the victims who suffered emotional and physical trauma, great pain and finally death. The victim's bodies were dumped in San Diego County as if they were nothing more than trash.

It's important to remember before their violent death, these victims were someone's daughter, mother, sister or wife. They were all human beings.

Jane Doe #1(20's) June 2, 1985. Was found 440 yards East of State Highway 94 at Steele Canyon Road in the Town of Jamul, California. The skeletonized remains were found by a woman hiking in the area with her dog when the grisly discovery was made. The hiker noticed bones one or two months prior but wasn't close enough to see if it was human or not. The remains found in an open area were a human skull with the lower mandible missing. The mandible was missing upper front teeth. There was a great defect in the occipital area of the skull due to blunt force trauma. The right tibia, fibula and foot were found intact inside a brown suede knee high Imperial brand women's boot with a pointed toe and a high heel. The boot was a size 7B. A tailbone and numerous rib bones were found. Pieces of blue jean material were attached to the leg bones and the boot. The victim wore a red sweat-shirt with Carroll's Music Center on the front with "Sound Reinforced designed by Carroll's" on the back. Beneath the bones, was a brown leather belt with a large white oval metal belt buckle containing the words "Hesperia Wrangler's" with a picture of a male wrestling a longhorn steer. Digging down to a depth of 15 inches numerous vertebrae and a spent .22 caliber bullet casing were found. A femur and rib bone were found 100 feet from the body, suggesting local wildlife were involved. A small amount of medium-length brown straight hair remained on the skull and some was found just south of the body. Based on the size of her femur, the victim was between 5'2"-5'3". She most likely died due to blunt force trauma to the skull cap area and the floor of the skull near the eyes, ears, nose or neck at the base of the spine.

There is an update to this case. There seemed to be enough information in the Coroner and Autopsy report to see if Jane Doe #1 could be identified. On Thursday January 31, 2019 while working on Jane Doe#1, after closely reading both reports, I found information which may lead to the identification of Jane Doe#1's skeletonized remains. The report stated "Jane" was wearing a brown suede Imperial Brand knee high boot with a high heel in size 7B. I checked online and found the Hesperia Wranglers was a family club founded on October 24, 1958 and still exists today.

After trying unsuccessfully to reach any club officers, phone numbers were either disconnected or the person was deceased. There was only a P.O. Box for address information. I called equestrian centers and tack shops and finally obtained a phone number for Tom and Toni Mustaikis. They advised me the belt buckle was not sold but was awarded once annually at the end of June to only male participants. So, the belt buckle either belonged to a boyfriend or husband who gave it to the victim or, a father who gave it to his daughter.

The club kept yearbooks going back to the mid 60's when they started giving this award. When asked if they knew of anyone from the area dropping out of sight during that time, they responded in the negative. Jane Doe#1 was found June 2, 1985 so since the award was given in the last week of June every year it must've been given before 1985. The silversmith who made the buckle moved his business to Apple Valley in 1982 and soon after started making the buckles for the Wrangler's. The owner, Dan didn't have a picture of his work available. This left it to 1982-1984 for the winner of the award. There appeared to be no press involved and the Mustaikis' were going to contact other members who might provide additional information.

On February 4, 2019, I contacted a Lieutenant friend with the San Bernardino Sheriff's Department and requested his assistance in checking with the Department of Justice to see if they could check missing persons with Jane's description.

In 1985, at the time her remains were found, the San Diego Coroner's office should've included this information when it was fresh and entered her information in the DOJ computer. I know the chances of solving her murder are slim to none, but I'm sure it would be comforting to the family of the deceased to reach some closure.

Donna Marie Gentile: Age 22, June 23, 1985. Gentile was found in an open area at the back of a turnout two miles North of Interstate 8 and 300 yards southwest of Sunrise Highway. Her neck and back were broken in several places and she was beaten about the head and face. Rocks and gravel were found tamped down her throat. Gentile had a gold earring missing and sustained a bite mark to the body. She was found approximately one day after being dumped. Her Autopsy was sealed and no one including family members were able to read the full report.*

Maria R. August 15, 1985. A homeless person who used heroin occasionally and prostituted herself was living on the street when she met a black male. As they were talking, he offered her twenty dollars for sex. She accepted and they rode the bus together to his apartment on 51st Street near El Cajon Boulevard.

Once inside, the suspect paid her and they engaged in sex. Afterwards Maria R. was showering when the suspect put a rope around her neck and began strangling her until she lost consciousness. After regaining consciousness, he attacked her again and she lapsed into unconsciousness again. The suspect told her when she came to, he would let her go if she orally copulated him. Fearing for her life she obeyed and was forced to orally copulate. He took his money back and let her go.

Tara Simpson:(18) August 26, 1985. Simpson was found as a result of Fire Department responding to a dumpster fire behind a business, in the alley near 51st and El Cajon Boulevard. Simpson was a transient from Oregon. Her teeth were knocked out and her body thrown into a dumpster. The fire was set using an accelerant. The body was burned almost beyond recognition which made her body difficult to examine forensically. However, a traumatic injury to Simpson's nose wasn't caused by the fire. There was a large gaping wound to her abdomen and evidence of small hemorrhages (Petechiae) indicative of (Asphyxia) suffocation on the surface of her heart. No aspirated soot was found in the lungs suggesting she was expired prior to being burned. The presence of sexual activity was found on swabs of oral, vaginal and rectal swabs. Simpson's body contained cocaine and alcohol.

Marsha Shirlene Funderburk: (25) September 26, 1985. Marsha was a single, unemployed mother of two children, Jeremy five years old and Amanda five months old. Marsha was found 50 feet south of the intersection of Old Highway 80 and Crestwood Road over 25 miles from her last residence. She was found at 11:45 am by a Sheriff's deputy and Border Patrol agents who were dispatched to the scene. Marsha was found on her right side with her knees flexed. She was wearing a red plaid shirt, black T-shirt, blue jeans pulled down to her ankles and brown suede shoes. A scarf was wrapped around her face and neck.

The body was in a moderate to advanced stage of decomposition making it difficult to determine if trauma was present. A set of keys were found attached to a belt loop in the back of the pants. There was a zodiac tag for Leo along with 20 keys on three key rings and a small crescent wrench and a Smurf tag. The cause of death was undeterminable but suggested strangulation. Identity was established by Dental Records.

Patricia Smith: (31) September 11, 1985. Patricia was found stabbed to death and left in a Travel Lodge motel room on El Cajon Boulevard. She was a local prostitute. She sustained stab wounds to the heart, liver, spleen, abdomen and chest.

Trina Carpenter: (22) February 11, 1986. Trina Carpenter was found as a result of a dumpster fire in an alley off Altadena Street near Monroe Avenue. This dumpster fire was close to the area from a previous dumpster fire where a body was set ablaze six months prior. Trina was raped, strangled and stuffed into a duffle bag which was doused with an accelerant. She was an active prostitute with a five-day old warrant for prostitution and indecent exposure. Trina's clothes and purse were also recovered from the dumpster.

Cynthia Maine: (26) February 21, 1986. Cynthia Maine disappeared after being released early from jail by a Criminal Intelligence Lieutenant from the San Diego Police Department. Cindy was the sister of former San Diego Police Officer Mark Maine and the daughter of former San Diego Police Officer Kenneth Maine. She was in jail for writing bad checks and informed on Police Officers to get her release time shortened. She became involved with officers from the narcotics street team, was given a false I.D. and was used as an informant for a Defense employer. She became romantically involved with at least one officer and possibly others.

A Homicide Sergeant who was just transferred to Internal Affairs had his locker, car, desk and house searched where explicit photos of Maine were found. Her vehicle was found at the La Mesa El Torito Parking lot, a known hangout for Narcotics officers. Her body was never found and the authorities dragged their feet and refused to take a missing person's report. The detective from missing persons who took the family's call told them, "She's in Las Vegas and you don't want to know." After she became missing the detective, she had a romantic relationship with stopped coming around and refused to help in the search for her daughter. The family has a diary Cindy kept describing her relationship with the officer. The Homicide Task Force added Cindy to the list of victims.

Michele Riccio: (19) April 24, 1986. Michele a single woman was found at 9:40 am by an Orange Grove employee in Valley Center. She was wearing a pink tank top, blue jeans and two-tone light blue and dark blue athletic shoes. She was lying supine on the ground. Needles and syringes were found adjacent to Michele's right leg. A teaspoon with a dried yellowish substance was found partially protruding from Michele's left front jeans pocket. Michele was in a rehabilitation program at the McDonald Drug Program at Scripps Hospital in La Jolla two years prior to her death. Two days before Michele's body was discovered, she babysat for a friend she knew and told her in the morning she was going to see her mother in San Marcos. Her father Gerald Riccio spoke to his daughter and thought she last lived in San Bernardino. She confided to him a year before her death she was using "Crystal."

Detectives responding to the scene were unable to establish a Homicide occurred and based on their information determined she died of a self-administered overdose of amphetamines.

Later the Homicide Task Force reopened the case and investigated it as a possible homicide linked to the other killings.

Jo Ann Sweets: (34) May 9, 1986. Jo Ann was a resident of neighboring La Mesa and found in a dumpster behind an apartment building off 51st Street. She was clad in a brassiere and a blouse but was nude from the waist down. Jo Ann was killed by manual strangulation and sustained injuries to her face and neck. Her spine, clavicle and neck were broken. JoAnn was wrapped in a bed sheet and a mattress pad and was placed in two plastic garbage bags sealed with tape. The body was covered by an afghan in the dumpster. Cocaine was present in her system.

Carol Gushrowski: (26) June 30, 1986. Carol was married and the mother of two children. She was depressed and under medication when she disappeared. Her body was found July 22 almost a month after she was reported missing. Apparently, she was picked up while hitchhiking and her body was found in the same general area as the other bodies in the Buckman Springs area of East San Diego County.

JoDell Jenkins: (28) June 30, 1986. JoDell was a single woman living at an Encinitas motel. She was found nude and in a supine position. A necktie encircled her neck. She was a 10-year heroin addict. She entered a drug rehabilitation program approximately 18 months prior where she received Methadone for a short period of time. A year before her death she was involved in a motor vehicle accident where she was hospitalized for her injuries. JoDell continued abusing drugs during this time. The body was discovered in a brushy area partially down a canyon in Valley Center by two women while horseback riding in the area. Homicide Investigators were unable to prove a Homicide occurred and with no signs of trauma and no suicide note present, they ruled her death as an accidental overdose. She was identified by Dental Records.

Jane Doe#2: On July 22, 1986 the body of Jane #2 was found nude in an open area on a creek bank four tenths of a mile Southeast of the intersection of Old Highway 80 and Old Buckman Springs Road in the Town of Pine Valley. Jane's body was decomposed with a large part in a mummified condition. The body was in an unusual position as it slid down the creek bank and her head was lodged under a tree limb. Jane wore a thin gold wedding band on her left ring finger. Most of the hair which was sloughed off her head was of moderate length and brown in color. Jane wore pink nail polish on her fingers and toes. Jane's teeth were her natural teeth with dental restorations. Clothes were found in the area but were determined to not be Jane's. The cause of death was undetermined. Autopsy results indicate a female of four feet eleven inches tall and over 20 years old.

Jane Doe #3: On August 3, 1986. Jane Doe#3 was found 25 feet North of State Highway 67 six tenths of a mile South of Sycamore Park Road in the Town of Lakeside. A husband, wife and daughter collecting rocks discovered the remains and summoned the Sheriff's Department. Jane #3 was found supine on a bedspread, on an embankment with her head down and feet facing the roadway. A pink blanket partially covered the body. She was clad in a blue shirt dress, with a belt like cord circling her waist, a half-slip, red panties and brassiere size 36B. Jane wore red nail polish on her fingers only. She wore a metal ring on her left fourth finger and two rings on her right fourth finger. A bracelet was found on her right wrist with two cord like plastic structures. She was approximately five feet five inches tall, weighed about 102 pounds and was in her 30's. Jane sustained a gunshot wound to the left shoulder area with pellets found in her heart lungs and chest wall.

Theresa Marie Brewer: (26) August 3, 1986.Theresa was an unemployed registered nurse living with her mother in Southeast San Diego. She was found by two men whose vehicle overheated, and they stopped in the area to let their radiator cool down. While walking a distance to find a place to urinate, one of the men detected a foul odor and followed the scent until he found the deceased. He went home to Calexico and after telling his wife the next day, they called Calexico Police who notified the San Diego Sheriff's department. Theresa was found three miles East of Kitchen Creek Road and 173 feet South of Interstate Route 8. She was found in a fetal position lying on her left side. An electrical extension cord was wrapped around her body. Her exposed buttocks were resting on a piece of cardboard. Brewer maintained her original teeth with a gold crown next to a porcelain cap. Theresa's mother reported her missing three weeks earlier. Identity was established when Theresa's mother brought her dental records in for comparison. Theresa's ribs and hyoid bone were fractured. She also suffered a hemothorax possibly as a result of her ribs being fractured. The cause of death was from probable strangulation

Sophia Glover: (37) August 15, 1986. Sophia was found on a grassy parkway between the sidewalk and street, rolled in a blanket in the 2200 block of Madison Avenue about a block away from Mississippi Street. Glover was homeless and living on the streets. She may have been prostituting to survive.

Glover sustained severe trauma to the head, neck and chest. Cocaine was found in her system. A small amount of Spermatozoa was found on a vaginal swab taken from Glover's body. Both sperm and acid phosphatase, indicative of seminal fluid was found on an anal swab.

The amount of genetic material wasn't enough for testing. Sophia was raped and beaten before she was strangled.

The autopsy determined she died from Asphyxia due to manual strangulation. A neighbor found her clothing neatly folded and stacked in an adjacent alley.

Nancy Alison White: (22) September 1, 1986. Nancy was married to a Marine Corporal and was the mother of an infant son. Nancy was a stock supervisor for an office supply company in Santa Ana, California and lived in El Toro, now incorporated as Lake Forest, California. Nancy's husband Milton was an aviation ordinance technician assigned to the El Toro Air Base but was temporarily stationed in El Centro. On August 26, 1986, Nancy drove to El Centro in her 1974 Volvo to celebrate her second wedding anniversary with her husband. She spent the night with her husband and started driving home the following day. At 3:30 pm her Volvo began to overheat. She pulled into a map stop off Interstate 8 near Lakeside. She called a friend, but when they arrived from Orange County, her vehicle was there but she was missing. Nancy was found over 30 miles away on September 1, 1986 when two boys found the body in Carlsbad and summoned authorities. Nancy's body was found nude in a supine position in a raised dirt area by a clump of trees. She was six tenths of a mile South of Poppy Lane and 100 yards west of Batiquitos Drive. Her panties and brassiere were found extending from her rectum. Nancy was beaten and raped before being strangled. Her neck was broken.

Jane Doe #4: (Pala) October 1, 1986. Jane #4 was a woman of approximately five feet four inches tall with black hair. Her body was found in an open area three and two tenths miles north of State Highway 76 and thirty-one-feet East of Pala Temecula Road in the Town of Pala. Scientific reconstruction of the face was accomplished, and she was known as Pala Jane Doe. Jane was approximately 18 to 20 years old. She sustained a fractured clavicle and one ear and both breast nipples were criminally removed. There was a sub-lethal amount of

Methamphetamine in Jane's liver. She was clothed in a white sweater, blue and white striped pants and white boots. One boot was on Jane's left foot. The right boot was found dangling from a tree branch about 25 feet south of the body. The sweater was pulled up under Jane's lower neck. No undergarments were present. The body was covered in various tattoos from her breasts, thighs and buttock areas. On the left side of her body was a paper bag containing empty beer cans. Beer cans were also found under the body and near her right hand.

Bertha R.: October 16, 1986. Bertha R. was employed as a cook and wasn't a prostitute although she lived in a high prostitution area on El Cajon Boulevard. While in a phone booth trying to look up a phone number of a check cashing place, a black male drove up in a blue Datsun 280Z started a conversation and told Bertha, he knew the location of the check cashing place and offered to drive her. He seemed so nice. She accepted and when they got to the check cashing place, she was unable to cash her check as their system was down. The suspect told her to hang out with him and she agreed. He drove her to a home on Mississippi Street. Once inside the two smoked a Marijuana cigarette. While they were on a couch, watching television he asked Bertha if he would be too forward if he asked her to kiss him. Bertha declined the kiss and they continued to watch television. The suspect then suddenly grabbed her neck tightly from behind. He wielded a knife in one hand and told Bertha if she didn't do what he said he would kill her. He forced Bertha to remove her clothes and attempted to sodomize her. When he was unsuccessful at achieving penetration, he raped her.

As she got dressed, he went through her purse and stole $65.00 cash. After Bertha dressed, the suspect said, "I've got to find someplace to put you." The suspect took her back to his car and they drove to Fiesta Island off Mission Bay. Once there he told her, he knew where she lived and he'd kill her family if she reported the crime. The suspect forced her to orally copulate him in the car. After she was finished, they drove around the San Diego area. When Bertha said she was going to vomit he let her out of the car, affording her an opportunity to escape.

Karen M.: October 20, 1986. Karen was an admitted prostitute and was at 2900 Imperial in Southeast San Diego, the center of the City's rock cocaine traffic. The suspect pulled up in a Blue/Green Datsun 280Z He solicited her for an act of prostitution, and she agreed. Although her preference was to car date, the suspect said he had a house and drove her to a house on Mississippi Street. When they arrived, Karen told the suspect she had a bottle of Jack Daniels whiskey and offered him some. The suspect went into the kitchen to get a glass while she disrobed. When Karen asked about her payment, he put her in a choke hold from behind completely lifting her off the floor from her neck. The suspect was roughly six foot five and 300 pounds. He told her to do as he said, or he would kill her. She was beginning to black out, so she agreed. After the suspect released her from his choke hold, he forced her to drink a large glass of Whiskey, which made her sick.

Karen told the suspect she would do whatever he wanted and pleaded with him not to harm her. He forced her to orally copulate him; he attempted to sodomize her but was unsuccessful. The suspect tried several more sex acts and continued forcing her to drink more Whiskey. Karen eventually passed out and came to when she was found by a Marjorie Wilsie who came to the house to clean up after her mother-in-law's death two weeks earlier. The police were called but she was transported to a detox facility downtown. She told the officers she was raped but they didn't believe her.

Kecia Betts: (Gardner) (21) In November of 1986, Kecia was eight months pregnant when she accepted a ride from a white male with glasses driving a van.

She was quarreling with her husband and decided to leave him temporarily to live in Florida, with her grandfather. Kecia was carrying a bag of clothing, a walkie-talkie, a stack of country and western tapes and a radio cassette player. She rode with the driver till they got to the In-Ko-Pah exit near Imperial Valley to make a bathroom stop. The next thing Kecia knew she was being choked and heard the driver utter, "I've got a gun." Kecia lost consciousness. When she awoke the man and the van were gone. Kecia walked to the other side of the highway and summoned help.

Jane Doe#5: December 5, 1986. Jane#5 was found by a maintenance worker at a rest stop in Oceanside, California. The location was two tenths of a mile South of Las Pulgas Road. The body was dismembered and contained nine body parts stuffed into trash bags at the stop. Authorities responded to a report of "body parts found" at the rest stop. At Autopsy, the bags were opened and examined in the presence of Sheriff's Homicide Detectives. The method of dismemberment was accomplished using a dull and sharp tool. A cause of death could not be determined due to multiple dismembered body parts.

Melissa Gene White: (22) December 31, 1986. Melissa was a single unemployed woman. She was found 20 feet North of State Highway 76 and one and two tenths of a mile East of Lilac Road in the Town of Pala, California. Melissa's body was found nude in a culvert. She was supine on the concrete floor against the South wall of the culvert. Her left eye protruded from its socket and the right eye was absent. A white, cloth-type belt was tied around her neck and across her open mouth. The belt was knotted in the front of the neck. A ¼-inch thick piece of braided line was also tied around the neck and knotted on the right side of the neck. Indentations from the belt and line were present on her neck and across her open mouth. The line led from the knot on the side of the neck and was tied around her left wrist and knotted. Melissa wore a white Ivory-like ring on her right middle finger and a white metal ring with one black stone and six white stones on the left ring finger. She displayed several tattoos: Over the pubic hairline is a tattoo of two roses, On the anterior aspect of her right shoulder was a crescent and star. Over the right scapular region was a crescent moon cartoon face.

Over the left first metatarsal there is a tattoo which reads "Punk" with a question mark or exclamation point. A vaginal smear indicated Spermatozoa heads and occasional intact Spermatozoa present. An anal Smear indicated Rare Spermatozoa heads present. Oral smear showed no Spermatozoa present. Identity was established by identification of tattoos of the decedent's mother along with fingerprint identification by Sheriff's Department. The cause of death was due to Ligature Strangulation associated with Morphine Intoxication.

Delores Fernandez: December 29, 1986 Prostitute Delores Fernandez was picked up by a suspect at Eighth and Hill Street in the City of Oceanside. The suspect drove to the parking lot of a nearby bowling alley and agreed to pay Delores $50.00 for oral sex. After Delores began the sex act, the suspect started choking her with his hands. Delores began to struggle and asked the suspect why. he was doing this. The suspect said, "He had to do it." Delores couldn't breathe and asked him again why and he told her the same thing, "He had to." Delores bit the suspect and escaped. Delores gave authorities a good description of the suspect and vehicle.

Juliana A. Santillano: (25) January 9, 1987. Juliana was found nude lying prone on a slight hill approximately five feet east of the parking lot at the Bird Sanctuary, South Bay Marine Biology study area in Coronado, California. She was last seen at Christmas by family. She called on New Year's Eve, but they hadn't seen or heard from her since. Juliana had two tattoos; one on the dorsal side of her left thumb with the name "David. "On the right shoulder was the name "Alberto." Juliana was a frequent user of Heroin and both arms exhibited track marks. The cause of death was determined to be by acute morphine poisoning. The death was classified as an accident.

Volah Jane Wright: (37) April 9, 1987. Volah was an unemployed, divorced single mother with a son living in San Antonio, Texas. Her body was found on Interstate 8, eight tenths of a mile east of the Camino Canada undercrossing. Volah was found in a semi-crumpled position on a grassy hill South of Interstate 8. The upper torso rested against a bush and her blackened head was downhill toward the highway. Volah was wearing white Aviva athletic-style shoes, white shorts with blue stripes, a black swimsuit with possible turquoise shoulder trim and possibly a grey slip or shirt. On the road shoulder close to the asphalt curb were two apparent blood stains with tire marks through the blood. It appears Volah may have been dragged a distance after being struck by a vehicle. Her skull was crushed.

Rosemarie Ritter: (29) April 23, 1987. Rosemarie was a single, unemployed beautician. She was an active prostitute in the early 1980's and was placed on geographic probation by the Honorable Judge Robert Cooney.* Her body was found 35 feet South of Interstate 8 and three and two tenths miles east of Jewel Valley Road in the town of Jacumba, California. Rosemarie lived at a large apartment complex on Madison Avenue in the Normal Heights area of San Diego. She was found nude in a prone position on a rocky hillside by illegal immigrants moving through the area. They stopped at a house and notified the residents who summoned authorities. There didn't appear to be any trauma to the body. Her hair was a dark brown, long and wavy, with the tips a reddish brown. Her nails were painted with hot pink nail polish on both hands and toes. With no fractures or trauma after toxicologically tests were taken, the cause of death was determined to be acute Methamphetamine Intoxication.

Rhonda Lynn Hollis: (21) May 10, 1987. Rhonda was a single, unemployed mother of two small children whose whereabouts were currently unknown. Rhonda was found in the 3600 block of Valley Road in the Town of Bonita, California in an unincorporated section of South San Diego County. Rhonda was found by joggers in the area. She was wrapped in a yellow, blue and orange quilt patterned blanket with a yellow border and bound with a yellow rope bound around her neck and feet. The body was in a fetal position within the blanket. The blanket wasn't removed and she was transported intact to the Coroner's Office. The blanket was blood soaked on the right side. Rhonda was in her 20's with light brown hair, brown eyes and was approximately five foot four and one-half inches tall. Her clothing included a pair of blood saturated light blue shorts and a black midriff cut T-shirt which was pulled up above her breasts. She also wore ankle length black mesh stockings. Rhonda wore a yellow metal ring on her left ring finger and a yellow metal chain with a "Foxy Lady" pendant and a white metal earring with multiple clear stones. Rhonda had blood which had dried on both her face and upper body. Her hands were bound at the wrists with the same rope binding her in the blanket. Rhonda's knees were pulled up to her chest with her left knee between her hands. A thin line was wrapped around Rhonda's neck and extended down to and around her upper legs. Rhonda sustained several puncture wounds to her mid chest area. Ligature marks were noted around her neck. Her left hand showed two unidentifiable tattoos and a rose tattoo on her left breast Her fingernails were neatly trimmed, and her ears were pierced with six holes in each ear. Her eyes showed signs of Petechial Hemorrhaging. Of the stab wounds she sustained the deepest was at a depth of six inches. The cause of death was stab wounds and Asphyxia by ligature strangulation. There was perforation of the lungs, the pulmonary artery and esophagus.

Anna Lucilla Varela: (32) June 22, 1987. Anna was a single, Hispanic woman from Lakeside California. She was employed as a kitchen helper at Edgemoor Convalescent Hospital in Santee, California. Anna's body was found in an open area nude in a prone position. Her feet were three-and one-half feet from the road bed of Old Highway 80 and one was nine tenths of a mile east of Sunrise Highway in the Town of Pine Valley, California. Her head was facing down the embankment and when found, her body was still warm to the touch. No identification was found on or near the body. Petechial hemorrhages were found in Anna's eyes and the upper portion of her chest. Anna was five feet three inches tall and weighed 194 pounds. On her inner left arm was a tattoo of the name, "Angel" as well as two birds, a rose and a scroll. Firefighters jogging in the area made the discovery. Anna showed bruising on the left side of her forehead and had a scar on the inside of her arm at the joint consistent with track marks. Anna also sustained extensive hemorrhaging on the right side of her neck. She had shoulder length brown hair and brown eyes. A computer check of the tattoo revealed a name and address. She was positively identified by fingerprints on file with the Sheriff's Department. The cause of death was strangulation.

Vickie Eddington: (29) July 30, 1987. This case started out as a missing mother of three married to a Navy Lieutenant Commander. Her vehicle was found with a flat tire, abandoned four miles away from the house the following day by her husband. According to her husband Leonard, she left that night for a nursing job and never arrived.

This case was originally assigned to Tom Streed who later was transferred to the Metropolitan Homicide Task Force. It wasn't followed up on until four and one-half years later.

Sally Moorman-Field: (19) September 20, 1987 Sally's body was found nude in a field off Sunrise Highway and two miles north of Interstate 8 in the town of Pine Valley, California. Sally was found by bicyclists in the area who notified authorities. She was the mother of one son. She had contacts with the Sheriff's Department for Prostitution and Drugs. Sally was strangled.

Sara Gedalcia aka Sara Finland Thornton: (36) September 25, 1987. Sara was a divorced woman writer, who resided in the City of Lemon Grove, California. She was found twenty feet east of Arnold Way and approximately 200 yards South of the intersection of Arnold Way and Alpine Boulevard, in the Town of Alpine, California. Sara's nude body was discovered by a person walking in the area. She wore a yellow metal ring and yellow metal bracelet that were left on the body.

Sara's skull was largely skeletonized and was in an advanced stage of decomposition. Sara exhibited two tattoos, one on her right shoulder which reads, "No Regrets." The other tattoo on the back of her right hand was of a long-stemmed rose. The identification was made by fingerprints, through the Sheriff's Department. Her brother David was in Wooster, Ohio and added, Sara suffered from Epilepsy. The Coroner listed the cause of death as Undetermined.

Unidentified Juvenile: October 1987. A juvenile prostitute was picked up expecting to perform an act of prostitution with the driver. After driving to the Pine Valley, area she was violently choked and threatened with a knife. Half-naked, she managed to escape and summoned help.

Diana Gayle Moffitt: (20) October 19, 1987. Diana was an unemployed dancer formerly from the Portland, Oregon area. She left the state with a boy-friend/pimp named Adrian Coleman. She was dependent on him for drugs and they had a rocky relationship. She eventually found her way to San Diego. Her mother searched the streets of Portland looking for her and placing flyers out. After dropping out of sight in San Diego, her mostly skeletonized body was found twenty-six feet southeast of the 9600 block of Blossom Valley Road in the unincorporated area of El Cajon, California. Diana was unearthed when two county road employees were cleaning out a drainage ditch when their skip loader uncovered Diana's body. Her skull and mandible were intact. A small amount of thin brown thin was seen on the skin. Both hands were found. She last wore a straight-legged, elastic-waisted pair of red pants. A brassiere which snapped in the middle with two snaps. It was fastened in back and a floral pattern was sewn on the front. All bones appeared intact showing no trauma or fractures. One kneecap was absent. All the bones were stained yellowed from administered doses of Tetracycline. Her teeth were all intact with some restorations. She was identified by dental records.

Donna Abbott/Robin Brown: February 1988. Abbott and Brown were friends and were hitchhiking to Tucson, when a driver picked them up and told them he could take them as far as El Centro. The driver mentioned he was released from the Marine Corps back in 1968. After stopping for gas, he pulled over for a bathroom break and started to choke Abbott who was positioned in the back seat of the vehicle. After Abbott was choked unconscious the driver choked Brown who was sitting in the front seat. One of the girls got away and ran for help. Her friend was found alive a short time later.

Betty Bass: March 1988. Betty was a homeless woman with a history of mental problems, she accepted a ride from a driver. After getting into the vehicle, the driver drove out to the east county where on the guise of pulling over for a restroom stop, he choked Betty until she lost consciousness. Betty survived the attack, walked to the roadway and summoned help.

Cheri Lee Galbreath: (25) April 13, 1988. Cheri wasn't identified at the time of her discovery and was originally listed as a Jane Doe. Her nude, decomposing remains were found in the 10900 block of Black Mountain Road in the Rancho Bernardo area of San Diego.

Years later she was identified by the Cal-ID fingerprint identification system which was a newly operational San Diego Database. Cheri was a transient from the State of Florida and didn't show a permanent address in San Diego.

Maria Weidmark: May 1988. Maria was a married woman living in El Cajon, California. After an argument with her husband, she decided to leave and was hitchhiking along Interstate 8 when a driver pulled over. She accepted a ride from the driver who said he could take her as far as El Centro. The driver asked to stop at a Buckman

Springs hang-gliding shop. Before they arrived, the driver choked Maria until she lost consciousness.

Melissa Sandoval: (21) May 29, 1988. Melissa was a prostitute who ran afoul with the law. Her nude body was found on Black Mountain Road in the Rancho Bernardo area of San Diego. Melissa was killed by strangulation.

Irene Quinland: June 1988. Irene was an active prostitute working on El Cajon Boulevard. While in the 4200 block of El Cajon Boulevard she accepted a ride from a white male driving a White Ford Bronco. She was driven to an area of the San Diego River underneath Interstate 805. The driver produced a shotgun and stated he was going to kill her. The driver instructed Irene to lay down in the back of the Bronco with a quilt blanket over her. Quinland managed to escape when the driver started up the car.

Irene May: (23) June 26, 1988. Irene May was tortured, stabbed to death and injected with battery acid. May was a married mother of three children and was estranged from her husband. Her body was never found. The murder occurred in the Live Oak Springs trailer park in the East County Town of Boulevard, California. This wasn't part of the murder series but was looked at by the Homicide Task Force because it was so compelling.

Sandra Cwik: (43) July 21, 1988. Sandra was a transient from the State of Florida. Her body was found in the area of Buckman Springs, California, where so many other victims were found. A blood trail almost a mile long was left with Sandra's footprints. Cwik survived the attack but bled to death attempting to locate help. She was beaten and her vagina was lacerated by a foreign object.

Annette Russell: (30) October 1988. Annette was a prostitute who accepted a ride from a driver who said he could take her as far as El Centro. On the way, the driver stopped at the same Buckman Springs exit and choked Annette into unconsciousness.

Cynthia Lou McVey: (26) November 29, 1988. Cynthia was a married woman from Livermore, California who recently entered San Diego County looking for employment. She was found nude, hogtied, gagged and strangled near the Pala Indian Reservation, in the Town of Pala, California. She was hoping to gain employment as a card dealer at one of the casinos. Cynthia was known to be involved with prostitution and drugs. She showed high levels of methamphetamine in her system. She was last seen at a Carlsbad Bar the previous evening.

Nicolette Jean Frye: (22) July 13, 1989. Frye was found bound, but fully clothed in a remote ravine in the 9400 block of Edgewood Drive in the Casa De Oro / Mt. Helix area of La Mesa. She was killed approximately three days earlier.

This is the most complete list I've accumulated regarding the victims The Homicide Task Force Investigated from September 1, 1988 to March 24, 1993, when a press conference was held.

CHAPTER EIGHTEEN

SEARCH WARRANTS AND SUSPECTS

PROSTITUTES dead and dumped in San Diego County. Meth-amphetamine dealers and snuff films. Prohibitive mailings, Murder for Hire and Bizarre Sex Acts. What the hell was going on?

Between 1985 and 1993 these cases were scrutinized and investigated by the San Diego Metropolitan Homicide Task Force.

If you recall, I put together a suspect for the Gentile murder and other cases involving Ronald Elliot Porter from October of 1988, when he was arrested for an attempted murder. I developed and provided it to Deputy District Attorney Dick Lewis and scheduled a meeting on January 14, 1989 * with Task Force Detectives David Ayers and his partner Gary Murphy. Among those present at the Saturday meeting was my Attorney Don Peterson and Lewis from the District Attorney's office. This meeting took place at Peterson's office in the Old Town area of San Diego.

In February of 1990, a report came back from the Task Force.* At the time of this report, the Task Force was under Deputy District

Attorney Bonnie Dumanis. Dumanis mentioned there were no suspects in the Gentile killing.

Porter was put on a back burner until Richard (Dick) Lewis took over the Task Force in October of 1990 despite Porter being arrested in October of 1988, convicted and sentenced for the attempted murder of Annette Russell. Somehow kidnaps, assaults and attempted murders didn't rise to the level of notice for the murders until after Lewis came to the Task Force. He went back and looked at deaths the coroner's office previously called "of undeterminable causes" and reinvestigated these cases. He was unhappy with the current practices of the coroner's office.

During this period there were thoughts the Green River killings in Seattle might be connected. Investigators were sent to the State of Washington to compare notes. By all accounts the media was already making this suggestion.

In January of 1984, I was sending information to the Green River Task Force on any prostitute I contacted in San Diego giving a Seattle address.* This was accomplished prior to any prostitute deaths in San Diego, so their Task Force could be alerted to their local prostitute movements.

One person, Richard Allen Sanders, a former law enforcement officer from a small town in Washougal, Washington was scrutinized closely by the Green River Task Force but was later determined to not be a suspect in any of their murders.

Sanders previously owned a Tavern in National City, a suburb just south of San Diego and made frequent trips from California to Washington. He dealt heavily in Methamphetamine and sold hard core pornography and "snuff films" according to informants. A "snuff film" means the people performing in the film are actually killed or snuffed out. Two informants claimed to view films featuring a woman and a small child and the child was killed. Additionally, in another film a woman and small boy are portrayed and the boy was killed. A third film was of an elderly man in a rocking chair. In the film he's shot in the head and his body slumps over to one side.

The informants only known as AAA and BBB indicated Sanders possessed these films locked in his Attic storage facility in El Cajon. The informant also mentioned he possessed photographs of women and recognized one of them as Melissa Sandoval, one of the Task Force victims. Members of the Task Force put Sanders under surveillance.

Sanders realized he was being followed, turned his vehicle around in traffic aiming it in a head on collision position with his pursuers. He was subsequently arrested,

Sanders was well off financially, made bail and was released before the Task Force could search his storage unit. Having knowledge of Sanders release, exigent circumstances caused the Task Force to issue a search warrant for night service in the event Sanders returned and removed possible incriminating evidence.

Task Force investigators served a warrant on the Attic Storage facility located at Second Street and Lexington Avenue space B-56 on February 11, 1989.* Investigators searched for films the informants mentioned as well as photographs of women and, two file boxes marked "Seattle" files and "San Diego" files respectively. A beige Ford Bronco vehicle was also mentioned in the warrant.

Sanders didn't return to his storage facility. Instead he fled the jurisdiction. Almost a month later he was shot and killed in Yacolt, Washington March 10, 1989. It was later determined Sanders didn't figure as a suspect in the San Diego killings.

JAMES MORRIS JACKSON

On February 26, 1990 prostitute Michele Ann Davis was working just east of the downtown San Diego area in Sherman Heights, when she was approached by a black male in his 20's driving a white pick-up truck. The driver stopped.

Davis approached his truck opening the passenger door asked him if he was looking for a date; the street vernacular commonly used by prostitutes means, "Do you want sex for money?"

The driver said, "Yes."

Davis entered his truck and said, "I know a place where we can go and transact business."

The driver said he knew of another place he wanted to go. He drove to a parking lot off Golf Course Drive to the farthest end of the lot and parked. The driver told Davis to get into the back of his camper shell, which she did. He appeared to be familiar with this location.

The suspect handed Davis four dollars and leaned over possibly to kiss her.

Davis stated, "Four dollars wasn't enough and she wanted more money,"

The suspect then stated, "You're going to give me head twice." (oral copulation)

Davis replied, "No!" and pushed the suspect away.

The suspect pushed Davis down and began choking her until she lost consciousness. When she regained consciousness, her nose was bleeding and she had urinated in her pants. Davis pleaded with the suspect not to hurt her. "Oh my God, don't kill me, I'll do it, I'll do it," she cried.

The suspect forced her to orally copulate him.

Davis feared if she didn't comply, she'd be killed. When Davis finished the suspect pushed her away and leaned back on the bed of the truck.

The suspect told Davis he was sorry and didn't know what was wrong with him. He didn't know why he did this to women. He said he was sick and needed a doctor.

Davis was shaking and in so much pain the suspect carried her back to the front passenger seat. He drove her back to 25th and B Street and dropped her off. She waved down a motorist and asked him to write down the license plate of the suspect's vehicle. Then she walked a block to a fire station where the police were summoned. She provided the license plate information to the police which was written down incorrectly by the motorist.

Task Force Detective John Lusardi wrote down Davis' description of the suspect as a dark-skinned male, six feet tall, heavy set with a pot belly. He had brown hair and eyes and was wearing a brown Pendleton shirt and dark blue pants, possibly work pants.

The Department of Motor Vehicle search came back with a 1974 Datsun truck registered to a woman with the last name of Jackson to an address located on Chimney Rock Road in the city of El Cajon. Further information showed a ticket was issued less than ten days ago to a male named James Morris Jackson giving the same Chimney Rock address, The physical description on the ticket matched Davis' description of the suspect.

A surveillance of the Chimney Rock Road address was performed where Jackson was followed several early mornings to NAS North Island to the public works building. He remained there until 3:30 pm and then drove back to the Chimney Rock Road address.

A search warrant* was served on the Chimney Rock Road address. In the search, a plaid shirt and a pair of purple underwear was seized as well as articles for establishing dominion and control .

Jackson was arrested for false imprisonment, assault with intent to commit great bodily harm and forced oral copulation.

STEVEN LAWRENCE JAMES

Steven Lawrence James was a real class act and considered a viable suspect for the murder of Donna Gentile. In 1984 and 1985 he was a client of Gentile's and was listed in her trick book. He was a friend of Greg McClendon's. You may recall in Chapter Two, Greg was in my academy class. He was terminated as a police officer shortly after graduation in 1980 for an indiscretion with a female driver during a traffic stop. The termination was for good reason.

While working my area I occasionally ran into him. He seemed to be trolling around looking for women. I recall him hanging out at 7-Eleven® stores in the East San Diego area. His friends, Larry Thomas, Pat Renny and James congregated at the 7-Eleven® store in the 7000 block of El Cajon Boulevard. Renny worked as a clerk and Thomas worked for a towing company. I stopped Thomas* many times giving girls including Gentile and Laurie Porter a lift to get them off the streets and away from Law Enforcement.

On one of these stops, I arrested Laurie Porter when I discovered she had an outstanding warrant. That night I drove Porter off the Boulevard. She was no relation to Ronald Elliot Porter.

Renny witnessed James bragging about prostitutes administering enemas to him during unusual sexual encounters where he'd become completely submissive.

McClendon first introduced James to Gentile. Gentile would administer enemas to James as well and told everyone she knew about James' bizarre sexual tendencies . Gentile told McClendon that James exhibited kinky sex appetites. When James heard what Gentile said to McClendon, he became infuriated with her.

Larry Thomas said James would publicly humiliate and shame Gentile by calling her a bitch, slut and /or cunt and he'd attempt to grope her vagina while she was inside the 7-Eleven®. Thomas heard James say to Gentile, "You should've been dead."

James engaged in sexual activities with Gentile at his house and maintained a sexual relationship with her for nine to 12 months before her death according to Thomas.

In 1989, Task Force detectives interviewed McClendon. He told them Steven James had a girlfriend named "A" who scratched James' eyes once during a domestic fight. James got so angry with "A" he asked McClendon to throw acid in "A's" face. McClendon contacted the San Diego Police Department's Criminal Intelligence Unit. They opened a murder for hire investigation. McClendon, with the direction of police investigators continued contact and surveillance with James as they built their case.

James changed his mind about the idea of throwing acid in "A's" face and decided instead to kill her using silver nitrate in a sample douche powder. James purchased silver nitrate, a highly corrosive and toxic chemical if ingested and added it to a feminine hygiene douche powder product. Then, James mailed it to "A's" residence. The prohibitive mailing was intercepted by Postal Inspectors and Police Detectives. James was arrested and convicted of Federal mail fraud and sentenced to prison time and probation.

In 1988, when carrying out a search warrant at James' residence, postal authorities only confiscated homemade tapes. They didn't search commercially manufactured tapes as they were looking for "snuff film" material or, any films that might pertain to Donna Gentile or other known prostitutes. Upon returning to James address on April 6, 1990 years later, investigators found James had moved out of San Diego and relocated in Phoenix, Arizona.

In May of 1990, Pat Renny was interviewed by Task Force Detective

Dave Ayers. He learned Renny, a part-time clerk at the 7-Eleven® store at 7000 El Cajon Boulevard, met and befriended Donna Gentile. Renny also stated, he knew James and Gentile maintained a sexual relationship at James's home nine to 12 months before her death. He also knew James often made home videos of the girls he met.

Renny recalled one occasion where James gave him a ride to jail to assist in bailing Gentile out and James made a comment calling Gentile, "the crazy bitch."

On August 13, 1990, Task Force detectives contacted "A" who indicated she started dating James in January of 1986. They went through a stormy, tumultuous and at times violent relationship. "A" described James as a violent and bizarre person who became like a madman when angered. James hit her at times causing bruises and cuts. Once he injured her wrist which required her to seek treatment at the emergency room.

He enjoyed watching porno films and wanted "A" to participate in a ménage-a-trois with a third partner. James would sometimes set up his house so "A" was locked inside, unable to leave for as much as four days. Numerous times James threatened to kill her and then he attempted it with the incident where he mailed her silver nitrate laced douche powder.

James made "A" aware he and McClendon knew a prostitute named Donna and at times he tried to help Donna financially. James also told "A" he helped with Donna's funeral expenses. He stated to "A", he knew who killed her, but when "A" was interviewed she couldn't remember the story. She shared with Ayers that James favorite place was Heise Park in the Laguna Mountains and he kept files on people in his personal computer.

Next, Task Force Investigators interviewed "B" on December 11, 1990. She married James back in 1977. Their marriage lasted until

1981 and they divorced. In 1983, child support / visitation documents were filed in San Diego County Superior court, case D163125. His ex-wife stated in a declaration, James was emotionally unfit as a parent due to the unusual sexual acts he engaged in, which might have involved their child. "B's" declaration was both thorough and explicit. It involved "sadomasochistic behavior" where James derived sexual pleasure from either degrading or humiliating "B" or wanting to receive degrading or humiliating treatment from "B." The incidents she described involved "B" having sexual relations with men and later recounting them to James for his gratification.

James would accuse her of being a whore who picked up hitchhikers and had sex with them. Then, he would insist "B" administer an enema to James in a way which made him feel totally submissive. He finally reached a point where he was having sexual fantasies which included "B's" mother and their daughter.

Larry Thomas imagined himself as sort of a "father figure" to Gentile. He met her near the 7-Eleven® store at 7000 El Cajon Boulevard and did favors for her like fixing her car, providing rides and picking her up from jail.

On May 14, 1991, "D" was contacted by Detective Ayers. "D" told him her daughter was going to school in Phoenix, Arizona. She stated her daughter met James when he lived in Escondido. Their relationship progressed to the point of marriage. Recently, the relationship went sour however, and her daughter resorted to obtaining a restraining order. She was terrified James would cause her harm or worse. She told Ayers the problem between her daughter and James grew as a result of his sexual fantasies, his insistence on receiving enemas and his violent behavior. "D" said her daughter called her numerous times indicating she lived in total fear of Steven James.

On May 15, 1991, Detective Ayers contacted "E" in Phoenix, Arizona. She was uncooperative at the time and didn't want to provide detectives with any information surrounding Steven James.

She was aware of his past and knew he was now seeking help and was no longer a danger to her anymore. She had moved back in with him.

On August 29, 1991, Task Force investigators located "F" and learned in March of 1988, after hearing about James' arrest, "F" contacted Postal Inspector Tom Taylor. Taylor was advised "F" dated Steven James during 1984 and 1985. She wanted to provide some background information and she told Taylor when she started dating James, she lost both her job and her boyfriend. James befriended her and "F" became financially dependent upon him, finally moving in with him for a short time.

"F" stated James was controlling and possessive with multiple mood swings ranging from jealous and violent to being supportive. "F" recalled one occasion when James beat her up and choked her until she was unconscious.

James used and supplied others with marijuana and cocaine. He hardly slept and he often went to El Cajon Boulevard late at night to associate with prostitutes. James told "F" he knew a prostitute named Donna who was involved with several police officers.

James's sexual appetites were the same with "F" as with other women; seeking enemas from them. He wanted her to perform sex with both men and women while he'd watch. James told "F" his former wife Jill, was killed several years ago in Big Bear, California. Her car's brakes were sabotaged, and she drove uncontrollably to her death. He told "F" he had other women killed and would kill someone for five thousand dollars. He once admitted to "F" he killed a prostitute by choking her, but she didn't believe him. James told "F" he met prostitutes on El Cajon Boulevard by the "Tubs" bathhouse or the 7-Eleven® store at 7000 El Cajon Boulevard.

One incident that bothered her most was when James showed her a "snuff film." She was sure it was real. It was on a Maxell video tape and of poor quality. It depicted a pretty, white woman with dark hair.

Both her hands and feet were bound to the bedposts. The woman in the movie was having sex with a white man with white hair in his thirties who appeared to be enjoying himself. The man then took a bandana and began choking the woman for what appeared to be a long time. When she apparently was dead the movie suddenly ended.

At the time of her interview with Detective Ayers, "F" was still in fear of James and wanted nothing to do with him.

When James was first contacted by Detective Ayers, he told him he had Type O blood group and recently underwent a vasectomy so he would become sterile.

With the assistance of the Arizona Public Safety Department, Ayers got additional information on James which facilitated issuing of a search warrant on November 1, 1991. Despite James's violent and bizarre tendencies with women he was eliminated as a suspect in the Gentile killing or any murders being investigated by the Metropolitan Homicide Task Force.

CHAPTER NINETEEN

SCANDALS

During my five-year career in the San Diego Police Department, I was proud to wear the badge of an officer and serve the public. It felt good to be "right around the corner" when someone who couldn't protect themselves called for help.

However, I strongly objected to the fact I was working for a, "Do as I say, not as I Do," department. No upper-echelon officers seemed to lead with their example. Chiefs were quietly driven home after being stopped for a DUI. This was true with judges as well. City property was misused for personal use. Impounded evidence was used for the benefit of Chief Officers.

Everyone seemed to have something dishonest or illegal on one another. This made the daily operation work out of a shared sense of fear as opposed to out of mutual respect. It gave many people the feeling the most important objective wasn't about getting to the truth. The aim was if you scratch my back, I'll scratch yours. I'm sure the first questions raised in Internal Affairs investigations in San Diego included:

- Is he a company man (or woman)?
- Will he or she look the other way?
- Or, will he lie if necessary?
- If not, what do we have on him?
- Or, what does he have on us?

On page 234 and 235 of Former Assistant Chief of Police of San Diego, Norm Stamper's book, *"Breaking Rank"* book. He wrote about "raucous parties held in the Chief's Office on Wednesday evenings. The liquor impounded from arrests was removed from the Impound area by Chief Officials and they would have a little drinking party in the Chief's Office. Stamper described it as, "Pouring generous portions of Bourbon, Scotch or Gin and drink themselves silly." This happened numerous times. It wouldn't have mattered much if it only happened once. That would be like being "slightly pregnant." However, the parties were a weekly tradition. This was no way to lead by example.

I knew of Vice Officers who failed to impound their seized liquor who were suspended from duty. The department might've done more, except one officers would've played the race card and it would become front page headlines. Just another slap in the face for members of the "corner pocket," common slang for the Chief's office.

According to Stamper's book, Cal Krosch, Commander at the time, mentions to Chief Kolender at a staff meeting, "Not very long ago you forced one of us to resign because of his drinking, aren't we being a little hypocritical here?"

A case of "drinkers' remorse" I guess?

There were plenty of cases involving officers of all ranks who had porn on their computers. Some wore mirrors on their shoes so they could look up the dresses and skirts of woman detectives. Officers would put in overtime slips claiming to be teaching at the police academy when they were off doing something else. Stealing money from a division coffee fund was common. In one scam on the department detectives would take suspects on extraditions to other states, purposely miss their flight and obtain flight vouchers for future flights to be used by them personally on the city's dollar.

When Bill Kolender was Chief of Police, an officer friend arrested an I.R.S. agent for indecent exposure. He was told to his face by Kolender, when the arrest was pulled, "We have to cooperate with other agencies."

Another veteran officer with a drinking problem often came to work under the influence but he was protected by his Sergeant. The Sergeant claimed the odor associated with an alcoholic beverage was simply his brand of after shave. He was a good cop when sober, but a danger to all when he drank.

GRAPE STREET PARK MURDERS

On September 14, 1984, the first female San Diego Police Officer was killed in the line of duty. Kimberly Sue Tonahill responded to an officer's call for assistance in Grape Street Park. Once there, she encountered two adult men and two teen girls consuming alcohol in a parked vehicle who were stopped by Officer Timothy Ruopp. Tonahill contacted one of the male suspects and, as she was patting him down for weapons, he suspect pulled out a 9mm pistol and in seconds shot Tonahill at point blank range. Officer Tonahill was struck in her armpit, an area unprotected by her bullet proof vest.

After shooting Tonahill, the suspect turned his weapon on Officer Timothy Ruopp and shot him in the leg. Before Ruopp could return fire, the suspect ran over to Ruopp and shot him in the head execution-style.

Hearing gunshots, Officer Gary Mitrovich responded to the scene and was shot in his shoulder. Tonahill died en route to the hospital and Ruopp died two days later. Mitrovich recovered from his wounds. The two suspects involved were captured during search of the canyon.

The shooter, Joselito Cinco was tried and convicted of first-degree murder and sentenced to death. While on death row at San Quentin, Cinco hung himself.

Where was Tonahill's mindset at the time? Was she preoccupied with other thoughts? Did she drop her guard for just an instant? Officer Tonahill, still on probation, had a lot on her mind. She had recently attended a friend's funeral and received a less than satisfactory evaluation. She was still on probation after less than a year in the field.

Her evaluation indicated, she lacked aggressiveness and wasn't suitable for field work. This weighed on her heavily. She worried her childhood dream of being a police officer was in jeopardy.

After her death, her locker was broken into and her evaluation changed to show she was a fully competent officer. The problem was Tonahill had already showed her boyfriend, another officer, her evaluation and made copies. A fact the department didn't realize. In this case, a burglary was committed to cover up a possible lawsuit. Forget the fact two officers were killed in the line of duty, but the City's priority was to save money from a possible lawsuit at all costs.

JEANNE TAYLOR'S DIARY

"Get me cigarettes," he barked as he threw money at her.

"Call the garage and have my vehicle gassed up!"

"Go and buy popcorn for the office!"

"Deposit my paycheck in the bank for me!"

Assistant Chief Burgreen, brought City Video Equipment and countless rolls of film from the police property room to film a fishing show and used the City Xerox machine and postal meter to send out his Bass Fishing Club newsletters. This is what the citizens of San Diego were being assessed.

These were just some of the orders Officer Jeanne Taylor marched to while she worked in the Chief's Office. Taylor decided to document her experience and keep a daily diary* of the errands she ran for the Chief's she worked under between March 1980 and September 1981.

Taylor was injured in the field when a porch she was standing on collapsed. She was assigned to Homicide on light duty status; but was transferred to the Chief's Office. The Chief's promised her a detective position in Homicide and dangled the carrot in front of her never coming through with their promise. Instead they treated her like a slave.

Running personal errands on city time, using city Vehicles and city gas. Discussing the entire diary would be time-consuming so, I'll mention some of the most outstanding entries:

March 28, 1980: Took Clyde Leach from his Lemon Grove home to the Kelley Pet Hotel on Morena Boulevard. Picked up his Great Dane Dog, stopped at Pet Store in Mission Hills for a 25 lb. bag of dog food then drove Leach and his dog back to Lemon Grove.

April 3, 1980: Sergeant Schroers advised me I couldn't attend the Homicide Convention at the Hilton Hotel April 1, and 11, 1980.

April 4, 1980: Picked up 25 lbs. of dog food at Pet Store in Mission Hills then drove to Lemon Grove to pick up Clyde Leach and his Great Dane. Took the dog and dog food to Kelley's Pet Hotel on Morena Boulevard and took Clyde to Sharp Hospital.

April 16, 1980: My academy classmate Joe Christianziani wrote a Traffic Citation to a friend of Chief Kolender's. (Ron Reina) It was

ordered pulled by Kolender and dismissed by his Traffic Captain, Pat
Rose.

May 1, 1980: Noticed Inspector Kennedy and Deputy Chief
Reierson went to a Padre game on duty and took no time off. Chief
Burgreen went fishing all day and took no time off.

May 2, 1980: Picked up Deputy Chief Stamper's overcoat at the
airport. He left it on the plane.

May 7, 1980: Per Chief Kolender's direction, picked up letter from
Jackson & Blanc @ 1970 Columbia Street and delivered it to Councilman Bill Lowery.

May 28, 1980: Picked up lunch for Chief Reierson and seven others
at Jurgenson's downtown.

June 18, 1980: Went to San Diego Office Supply for Chief Stamper
to pick up felt pens.

June 19, 1980: Went to San Diego Office Supply for Chief Stamper
to pick up Notebooks.

June 24, 1980: Xeroxed from 1:30pm to 4:45pm for Chief Nyhus.
(Police Olympics)

June 25, 1980: Xeroxed from 10:15 am to 12:15 pm for Chief
Nyhus. (Police Olympics)

July 9, 1980: Chief Reierson threw a ten-dollar bill at me and said,
"Get me change and cigarettes."

July 14, 1980: Took a Bar Mitzvah Gift to Post Office for Chief
Kolender.

July 16, 1980: Picked up Round-Trip tickets to Las Vegas for Chief
Kolender from Steve Gardella, Vice president of Security for Pacific
Southwest Airlines.

August 4, 1980: Picked up Chief Kolender's Charger Tickets from Joe Scott at Charger Stadium.

August 8, 1980: Picked up cigarettes for Chief Reierson.

August 19, 1980: Took Dennis Kolender(son) from police department to home then to Orthodontist then back to Tierra Santa home.

August 21, 1980: Picked up gun at pistol range for Chief Kolender from Ann Williams.

August 21-31, 1980: Under doctor's care at Kaiser Hospital -No Work-

September 10, 1980: Picked up Chief Kolender's girlfriend at her home in El Cajon and brought her downtown for their date. Lois Karas widow of San Diego Charger Emil Karas.

September 16, 1980: Took Ticket Issued to Ron Reina to Captain Rose to be fixed. Ticket #0871676

October 6, 1980: Picked up Phil Del Campo (Personal friend of Chief Kolender) at his home and took him to the Police Pistol Range for a steak fry.

October 8,1980: Dropped off wine decanter at Mayor Pete Wilson's office. Chief Kolender and Mayor Wilson each received this gift from a Mexican Official.

October 10, 1980: Took Dennis Kolender to Orthodontist in La Mesa then waited to take him home to Tierra Santa.

October 15, 1980: Paid car payment for Chief Kolender at San Diego Trust and Savings. ($67.87)

Oct 21, 1980: Pick up Dennis Kolender at High School and took him to the Dentist. Had tooth pulled then took him home. (three hours)

October 30, 1980: Picked up Chief Kolender's Halloween Costume.

November 19, 1980: Went to 10th and Broadway to have Chief Kolender's electric razor repaired.

November 25, 1980: Gave Sergeant Schroers my Investigative transfer request. He was aloof and cold toward me.

December 1, 1980: Sergeant Schroers gave me a denial for the Investigative list.

December 2, 1980: Took Randy Kolender to Dr. Heston Wilson, Otolaryngologist, for a 2pm appointment. Drove from Downtown to Tierra Santa, back Downtown then back home then back Downtown.

December 5, 1980: Deposited Chief Kolender's personnel paycheck.

December 15, 1980: Drove to 9404 Genesee Road to pick up Charger tickets for Chief Kolender from Henry Summers. (Real Estate Developer)

December 16, 1980: Picked up lunch for 20 people at Jurgenson's downtown. Picked up two Charger /Steelers tickets for December 22, 1980. Sec 5 row 4. Picked up two tickets for Chief Kolender to Helen Copley's dinner (Owner of the San Diego Union Tribune) tonight at the Hotel Del Coronado from Janice at Mayor Wilson's office.

December 18, 1980: Went to Grand Prix and sold two Charger/Steelers tickets to Rita Hunt for twenty-four dollars.

January 7, 1981: Assistant Chief Bob Burgreen gave me my grievance back. (denied)

January 23, 1981: Went to the Police Pistol Range for Chief Kolender to pick up a package of .38 caliber shells. The shells were for Chief Kolender's friend John from the Old Ox restaurant.

January 27, 1981: Sergeant Schroers told Captain Williams how much work he had to do. Captain Williams said, "You have a Gopher over there." "Make her do the work."

February 6, 1981: Set up two free passes for Marilyn Kolender at Sea World.

February 18, 1981: Drove out to Suzanne Thompson's house in the College area and picked up a painting of Chief Kolender. The painting was so large had to drive back downtown and use a Community Service Officer Van to transport.

February 25, 1981: Picked up a package for Chief Kolender at the security gate of Pacific Southwest Airlines off Carroll Canyon Road at 10:30am. Chief Kolender said he lets me do things like this because he trusts me.

March 3, 1981: Took the large picture from Chief Kolender's office to his Tierra Santa home in Community Service van.

March 7, 1981: Captain Williams gave me my rejection for my request to get on the detectives list.

March 19, 1981: Chief Kolender was at the Westgate Hotel getting haircut. He told me to bring him his checkbook, as he had no money.

March 27, 1981: Deposited the Chief's checks to their respective banks.

April 1, 1981: Dropped off a gun to Frank Curran at the Charger's Office. Collected a check for $233.20.

April 16, 1981: Assistant Chief Bob Burgreen sent out his usual news letter to all his Fishing Club members. All letters put into City Envelopes and Postage paid for by the City.

April 17, 1981: Perfect example of going nowhere. Two Officers hired after me go to detective assignments.

April 23, 1981: Picked up rolls and rolls of film from the police property room for Chief Burgreen's Fishing Trip.

May 4, 1981: Delivered Lieutenant Grimm's and Colman Conrad's (Deputy City Manager) DUI arrest report to Ted Broomfield, (Deputy City Attorney) at the City Attorney's Office (trying to keep it hush hush.)

May 5, 1981: Chief Kolender's father involved in a misdemeanor hit and run accident downtown. Traffic Captain Pat Rose and Sergeant Schroers from Chief's office trying to cover it up.

May 8, 1981: Deputy Chief Reierson went fishing for a half day with Detective Gene Back. Left at 11:30am never came back to work, took no time off or vacation time.

May 8, 1981: Went to Chief Kolender's bank to get a $500.00 cashier's check. This was to pay off his dad's misdemeanor hit and run last Tuesday.

July 2, 1981: Chief Kolender asked me to pick up his dry cleaning and laundry.

July 2, 1981: Picked up three rolls of film for Chief Burgreen to take on his personal trips from the Police Property room.

July 21, 1981: Chief Kolender fixed his son Dennis' parking ticket.

July 21, 1981: Received rejection letter from the Retirement Board regarding my case. Checked out a Community Service Van and took the large painting of Chief Kolender back to the artist.

August 6, 1981: Picked up seven rolls of film for Chief Burgreen's next fishing trip from the property room.

August 7, 1981: Chief Kolender asked me to go to Webb's TV and pick up his home television. Chief Kolender asked me if I would ever go to the Civil Service Commission and tell what he had me do?

August 17, 1981: Deputy Chief Ken O'Brien asked me to call the garage and have them gas up his car.

September 1, 1981: Chief Kolender asked me again to promise I would never tell anyone about the errands I have to do for him.

September 2, 1981: Deposited $130.00 into Chief Kolender's checking account at San Diego Trust and Savings. (Seaport Village)

These were only some of the better entries. I apologize if this rundown of orders was monotonous for you to read. Consider what Officer Taylor felt like going through this type of daily abuse for 18 months day in and day out.

As a result of the news of this leaking to the press, both Chief Kolender and his Assistant Chief Bob Burgreen received notes in their file from then City manager John Lockwood.

In similar cities where this type of activity took place criminal charges were filed.

THE ROLODEX 500 FILE

A search warrant was served on Karen Wilkening in 1987. San Diego Police Detectives were attempting to seize the business records of her high-class call girl ring. Detectives followed her to a meeting and once outside, told her to follow them back to her condominium and open the door or they would break it in.

Once inside vice detectives search her condominium and found a rolodex file in a kitchen cabinet. This contained over 500 rolodex cards with the names of paying customers. Some names were of highly successful and prominent San Diego Businessmen, Athletes and Philanthropists

No arrest was made at this time, but anticipating going to jail, Wilkening failed to appear on the second day of her preliminary

hearing. Her former Defense Attorney Buford Wiley was instru-
mental in conspiring to obstruct justice by allowing her to leave the
country. A good friend of Wilkening from back east came to live a
short time with her and provided Wilkening with her passport.
Wilkening wore a wig and became Linda Webster for all intents and
purposes. She fled the United States for the Philippines. She
remained there from September 23, 1987 to May 10,1989 when San
Diego Task Force detectives brought her back to stand trial.

During the seizing of Wilkening's Rolodex file, there was no chain of
custody over it. Instead of being impounded and secured as evidence,
it sat on the Police Department's Vice Lieutenant's desk where all
who entered could see and tamper with it. The file was "sanitized"
with names removed, according to a vice officer who shall remain
nameless.

The purpose for bringing Wilkening back to the states was to determine if there was a connection between her and the prostitute
murders. Media reported the day before Donna Gentile went missing, she attended a party hosted by Don Dixon who paid Wilkening
for prostitutes from his failed Texas Savings and Loan. People at the
party stated Gentile was in attendance. Gentile attracted lower class
"customers" and she either went to the Johns place to conduct business, used a trick pad out of a motel or was a car whore. These were
two different classes of people. However, it was something the Task
Force needed to investigate and rule out.

Wilkening was tried and convicted of one count of pandering and
conspiracy to obstruct justice, for leaving the country.

One morning at breakfast with Dick, I was shown several sheets of
paper containing the names from the Rolodex file. The Rolodex was
now in the custody of the District Attorney's Office. The Homicide
Task Force was looking into it for the Grand Jury. I would've brought
a pad of legal paper if I knew, I would actually see this document.
Unfortunately, I only had napkins at the time to write on as fast as I

could before transferring them later to paper. I wrote down the names of the people I recognized. Some of the people mentioned in this list are referred to by description as opposed using their true names to protect their identity.

Bill Kolender's Barber

A sailor

A Police Officer

Donna Gentile's Property Manager

Owner of a Trucking Company

An Event Planner

Owner of a Leasing Company

A San Diego Philanthropist

A Real Estate Developer

A friend of Gerald Ford

Another Philanthropist

A Real Estate Developer

A Boxer's Manager

A Social Worker

A Mission Valley Property Manager

A Judges Father

A San Diego Defense Attorney

A Wrestler

A Former City Manager

A Baseball Coach

A Car Dealer in El Cajon

A Police Officer

Another Car Dealer

A Doctor

An Actor

A Campaign Contributor to Sheriff Bill Kolender

Another Real Estate Developer

An Insurance Broker

Another Philanthropist

Another Contributor to Kolender for Sheriff

A Tax Preparer

Another Attorney

A Salon Owner

A Doctor

Construction Owner

A Property Manager

A Business Equipment Owner

A Doctor

A Real Estate Developer

There were many more, but I think you get the idea of the diversity of the people who permeated the Rolodex.

CHAPTER TWENTY

STREED THEN GOUDARZI

AFTER THE GENTILE MURDER, there was an agency and media frenzy for a quick-fix solution to the case. People wanted and demanded answers. A lot of mistakes were made from the get-go which few people were aware of. At the crime scene, Sheriff's personnel, one of whom was dyslexic recorded all the readings incorrectly and they had to be reinvestigated.

Thomas Streed, was the initial Sheriff's Department homicide investigator, took only notes and didn't document his findings with any recorded statements from people. No one is perfect, but you must use whatever implements are available to memorialize the details over and above using brief notes and your memory.

There was a thirty-nine-month gap from the time of Gentile's murder until the inception of the San Diego Metropolitan Homicide Task force which came into existence on September 1, 1988. It was a well-known fact, the longer it takes to gather information at a homicide scene, your solvability factor geometrically increases.

In a television video, Streed pointed out all tracks were "brushed out" at the Gentile crime scene. So, immediately he determined the killer must be someone connected with law enforcement who would know what evidence to erase to avoid detection. His theory was a police officer was Donna Gentile's killer.

However, as a former Marine, Streed had the answer available on the tip of his nose but he couldn't see it. The "brush out" technique Streed referred to is also taught to all Marines during boot camp when they're introduced to anti-tracking techniques. Regardless of whether you are a cook, a radioman or infantry person they're all put through the same training. This is straight out of the Marine Corp Manual drummed into every soldier's head so powerfully, you can recite it backward and forward in your sleep. It should've presented a clue about what type of person to investigate. Several months before the formation of the Homicide Task Force Dick and I discussed options regarding who were the type of suspects capable of breaking necks and backs.

Digressing back to 1985, Streed asked me to come in and talk with him. I said, "Sure but I'll be there with an attorney and it's my right to do so."

Streed replied, "Then I don't want to talk with you."

I knew if I went and talked with him without an attorney, I'd never walk out a free man. Instead, the Sheriff's department illegally impounded my car with a hold for Homicide and made numerous false statements and omissions on Sheriff's traffic officer Blu's impound report.

Once on the Homicide Task Force, Streed was taken off the Gentile case and assigned to another team to investigate Police corruption. Other task force members considered him a "Maverick." I was told Streed didn't share information with Task Force members. If someone shared information with him that didn't fit the parameters of his theories, he'd disregard it. By this time, Chuck Rogers was elevated to the Municipal Court Bench as a Judge. Bonnie Dumanis took over as head of the Task Force. Her position lasted less than a year when she took on a position as a Juvenile Court Referee.

While there was a cloak and dagger operation going on since its inception, Task Force investigators weren't sharing information with each other and the program wasn't properly managed under Dumanis.

Streed and Goudarzi butted heads constantly and Streed resented the fact once again he had to run everything past Goudarzi.

On the other hand, Streed had tunnel vision when it came to who killed Gentile. Goudarzi was accused of being a mole for the department, reporting back to superiors what was going on in the investigation, a clear violation of Task Force policy. If they wanted to send the best, I could think of 20 other officers on the department they could've sent before ever coming to him. No, he was put in that role for other reasons. This wasn't just Streed's feeling, but many members of the Task Force saw it as well. All this dissention and lack of trust was going on during Dumanis' watch.

One morning while meeting Dick for breakfast, we were discussing Streed and his theories. Dick had heard just about enough stories regarding Streed.

When I mentioned Streed asked me to come in and talk to him about the Gentile case without an attorney and then the Sheriff impounded my car, which I lost to a lien sale because I couldn't pay the fees, he suddenly turned beet red.

Thinking Dick was choking on food, I got up from the table to use the Heimlich Maneuver.

Dick put his hands up saying, "No I'm all right, just pissed off. I'm going to make some calls when I get back to the office." The following day Streed was removed from the Task Force. I don't know who Dick called or what was discussed, but Streed was history. Dick was still working the Municipal Court and hadn't been assigned to the Task Force yet.

Goudarzi on the other hand was an odd duck. There were policing styles and then there was Goudarzi's. After working for 22 different Sergeants during my five plus years, nobody ever employed his style of policing. Most Supervisors are there to assist when called upon and provide guidance when necessary. But Goudarzi operated outside the norm. Supervisors aren't supposed to do a police officer's job. On several occasions, he'd beat us to calls and we'd arrive only to find a drunk he put to sleep and we'd be left with the cleanup. He didn't allow his officers to do their jobs and supervise us to make sure we did ours.

I spoke with Goudarzi once and said, "Look Sarge if you feel you're a frustrated Patrolman and miss the action so much, then take off your chevrons and join us. Otherwise, let us do our job."

Goudarzi was under a microscope by the department during the prostitution enforcement detail pressured to show high levels of activity since he was the Sergeant under Carl Black. He was hard on the squad to produce numbers so he would make himself look good. Field interrogations slips, tickets, arrests and the like. Many officers didn't care for his policing style either and talked about transferring to another squad. But when it came to my investigation when they were asked to speak to the Captain about their concerns, they preferred to either change their story or not speak up at all. They were intimidated.

Even Goudarzi knew Gentile was trouble. It was an established fact she was out to burn cops and she carried a tape recorder with her on some occasions. I believe this activity stems from the fact a law enforcement father figure molested her in Pennsylvania which led to her running away from home across the country to San Diego. This was contained in a probation report after she was arrested in San

Diego. Sure, every time she could burn a cop, in her way she was getting even with the man who molested her growing up. Knowing she carried a tape recorder at times didn't stop me from getting the information I needed from her to verify her claims regarding Lieutenant Black. All the better to record it.

After hearing Goudarzi speak about Gentile on the witness stand at my Civil Service hearing as the city's witness against me, he made positive remarks confirming what I knew about her capabilities to burn cops. I felt like things were moving in my direction. But, alas, I'd be proven wrong again. The department didn't want the truth. They were more interested in upholding their image. I was a mere "chip" and they let the chips fall where they may.

Goudarzi started running afoul of the department when he brought in a psychic by the name of Linda Davis. For professional purposes she used the name, Kelly Roberts. Goudarzi shared office space with her at her hypnotherapy business. In 1989, Goudarzi sold Davis a gun she couldn't afford to go out and purchase herself. She was making payments to Goudarzi to reimburse him. In September of 1989, after discussing divorce with her husband James C. Davis Jr. he attacked her with a baseball bat. She shot and killed him with the gun. Even though the sale of the gun was legal, it was one more thing which delayed a proper investigation by the Task Force when allegations of an affair between the two surfaced.

She claimed she was hired as a consultant for the Clairemont rape/murder series of six women as well as the prostitute murder series which happened between January and September of 1990. She was considered an informant and issued a code number. Chief Bob Burgreen knew nothing about it. This occurred during Bonnie Dumanis' watch.

In June of 1990, Goudarzi received a call from Denise Loche, a Mira Mesa housewife who claimed to have information on the Gentile case. This was supplied to her from an unlicensed San Diego Private

Investigator named Rick Post. He was in the Point Loma area of San Diego.

Post's name wasn't mentioned in the media, but one day I received a call from Mike Workman, the Assignment Editor for KNSD television, the local ABC affiliate station. I knew Mike when he was the Assistant Assignment Editor at KFMB television, the local CBS affiliate station since the Gentile investigation. Mike said, "Hey Larry, I'm meeting up with Denise Loche at the station tomorrow morning. Would you like to be here and meet with us?"

I told Mike, "Sure I'll be there." The next morning, I drove to the television station and met with Loche and Workman for about an hour. We touched on several topics and what she said about Goudarzi was both informative and enlightening. Loche claimed Goudarzi quickly went from Investigator to Lover. Loche also claimed she was asked to wear a wire and attempt to find out who was leaking information from the Task Force to the press. She was also asked to wear a wire into F.B.I. headquarters to find out if they were working the Gentile case. Why would Goudarzi care if the F.B.I. was involved unless he was checking it out for the department?

Loche claimed she was drugged and raped by Goudarzi at his apartment after smoking a cigarette she said was laced with something. Here we go again, folks. Precious time was taken away from properly investigating the murders in order to deal with this crap.

Dick told me Goudarzi told his partner, Jim Reynolds he had to see an informant (Loche) and left him behind. Goudarzi, during the investigation said he paid her out of his own pocket.

I told Dick a mouthful about Goudarzi and Dick replied he was up to here with him putting his hand over his head.

Dick told me Loche wasn't authorized to act as an informant. Secondly, Goudarzi violated policy regarding the payment of money where a second officer is always supposed to be present to verify the amount given to an informant.

Goudarzi was removed from the Task Force during an internal investigation and ultimately fired. This was a serious embarrassment to Chief Burgreen.

It was later determined Goudarzi's time spent with Loche was always when he was off duty, at his apartment on his own time. He received his full retirement after the Fourth District Court of Appeals overturned the lower court's decision in November of 1994. Hey, what's the old saying, (pardon my French) "You don't S—t where you eat."

Bob Burgreen was the current Chief of Police and he was concerned about early reports some of his officers could be involved in the Gentile and Cynthia Maine murders. In an attempt to douse any fires in that direction, he sent his second in command Assistant Chief Norm Stamper to the Task Force in June of 1990. Stamper's role was to overlook its operation and report his findings. He asked Goudarzi if he was involved socially with Loche, to which Goudarzi responded, "No." Goudarzi didn't remember him asking the question, but Stamper did.

All this soap opera drama happened before October of 1990 when Dick took over the Task Force. Dick wouldn't allow any crap on his watch. He was a man driven with a mission; to solve these murders and get dangerous people off the streets.

Incidentally, as a sidebar, years later in 1998, Rick Post was lured to Tijuana by his lover Kimberly Bailey and an associate. They hired a Mexican hit man who kidnapped and tortured Post for five days. Then he did away with Post. His body was never found.

Bailey thought Post was stealing money from their business. They sold machines that were supposed to emit electromagnetic waves or frequencies to cure a number of diseases. She also believed he was seeing another woman.

The associate rolled over on Bailey who was convicted and sentenced to life in prison. She was caught when the FB I used a former KGB operative, Svetlana Ogorodnikova, who seduced F.B.I. agent Richard Miller* of Valley Center into passing a secret document to the Soviet Union. Ogorodnikova was living at Bailey's Fallbrook Ranch home and befriended her. She wore a wire for the Bureau and recorded incriminating statements regarding Post's kidnapping, torture and murder for hire.

In September of 1990, Gary Schons from the California State Attorney General's office was also added to head up the Police misconduct investigation so as not to infer just cops were investigating each other. It wasn't something they enjoyed doing, nevertheless it had to be done.

In October that year, District Attorney Ed Miller moved Richard J. (Dick) Lewis to head the Homicide Task Force. In later years, when I discussed my role in the Task Force Investigation with Ed Miller, he told me he would've put Dick on the Task Force to start with, but he couldn't spare him away from the Special Operations Unit or the Municipal Court.

CHAPTER TWENTY-ONE

TASK FORCE ROGUES GALLERY

THIS CHAPTER COVERS both the suspects and their victims. These people were animals who created carnage toward their victims. Other than mentioning their name and how they were brought to justice, they require no additional notoriety.

Elmer Lee Nance was arrested for the rape and murder of Nancy Allison White. This case occurred prior to the existence of the Homicide Task Force on August 27, 1986 and was a Sheriff's Homicide case. White was beaten, raped and murdered at a map stop off Interstate 8 on her way back from celebrating her wedding anniversary with her husband. He was normally assigned to El Toro but was on temporary assignment in El Centro, California. White made the trip and spent the night with her husband. On her return home she experienced car trouble and pulled off the road. She called a friend to help and when he drove from Orange County to the map stop, Nance was there. White's vehicle was there but she was nowhere to be found. Nance had already raped and killed White at this point. The body was in the back of Nance's vehicle.

Days later, on September 1, 1986 her nude body was discovered 30 miles away near the Batiquitos Lagoon, in the City of Carlsbad. In 1990, Detectives Dan Hatfield and Ron Thill from the San Diego Police Department were assigned to the Homicide Task Force to investigate White's murder. Their follow up investigation showed Elmer Nance was a convicted sex offender who, resided in Barstow and failed to register. Barstow authorities were contacted but were unable contact him.

After some surveillance Nance was located and followed from his motel to a local store where he was arrested. Nance was interviewed and confessed to the crime. He was tried, convicted and sentenced to 25 years to life for the murder, with an additional five years to run consecutively for a violent prior arrest. Nance is now deceased.

Daniel Thomas Stafford: Stafford picked up a 17 year-old juvenile prostitute in October of 1987, drove out east with her and while she was expecting to provide sex for money instead, she was choked and threatened with a knife. She managed to survive, and Stafford was arrested for kidnapping. He was convicted on a lesser charge, was given credit for time served and placed on five years' probation by the Honorable Judge Bernie Revak.

Leonard Eddington II was a Lieutenant Commander in the Navy. His wife Vickie, mother to their three children was separated from her husband, who was living at his mother's house in 1987 when she was murdered and missing. The case was assigned to Tom Streed before being transferred to the Task Force. The case was left unworked until 1991 when it was given to Detective Dennis Brugos of the Sheriff's department. After looking at it, he felt there was so much information on the case, it became a Task Force case. Neighbors complained for years about Eddington using a bulldozer in his backyard and he kept people from going there. Brugos was concerned about the husband's demeanor throughout the case. After a flyover of Eddington's property, an area near a ravine appeared to be filled with dirt. A search warrant was served on the property and his wife's remains were uncovered. He was placed under arrest for the murder of his wife. On November 6, 1992 Eddington was sentenced to life without the possibility of parole.

He killed her out of greed. She wanted a divorce and he didn't want her getting anything.

Thomas Eastgate pled guilty to assaulting an unknown prostitute with a deadly weapon. He was convicted and imprisoned.

Terry Millaud was found guilty of the stabbing murder of prostitute Patricia Smith found in a Travel Lodge motel room on September 11, 1985. He was also linked to the stabbing murder of Charles Irwin at a San Diego South Bay Alpha Beta store. He attempted to carjack Irwin's wife's car. When she called her husband to the scene Millaud stabbed him to death on August 19, 1985. Millaud was apprehended and charged with multiple murder counts and robbery. Millaud was the last to occupy the hotel room.

James Morris Jackson was identified as the suspect in the false imprisonment, forced oral copulation and assault with intent to commit great bodily harm to Michele Ann Davis on February 26, 1985. After obtaining his license plate and identifying him as a suspect in the attack, detectives placed him under surveillance and followed him from his residence to work and back before obtaining a search warrant for his home. After obtaining evidence from his home Jackson was arrested in March of 1985 and charged with the above-mentioned crimes. (See Chapter 18: Search Warrants and Suspects)

Alan Michael "Buzzard" Stevens was located in San Marcos, California living out of his vehicle. After killing prostitute Cynthia McVey, print evidence on tape used to keep a sock gag in her mouth was left at the murder scene led authorities to Stevens along with other evidence found in his storage unit. He was tried and convicted October 31, 1990 for the November 28, 1988 murder and received a sentence of 25 years to life. Stevens died in prison.

Blake Raymond Taylor was identified by his victim as the suspect who forced her to get down in his vehicle at gunpoint and cover up. Taylor picked up Irene Quinland working as a prostitute, in the 4200 block of El Cajon Boulevard. Once inside, Taylor drove Quinland to an area underneath Interstate 805 in Mission Valley near the San Diego River and brandished a shotgun telling Quinlan he was going to kill her. He told her to get down on the floor area of his vehicle and cover up with a pad or blanket.

Quinland asked why he was doing this?

Taylor told her because he had to otherwise, she could lead the police to him, and they would find out about the other girls. He also asked her if she was going to cry and beg like the Mexican girl. This later led authorities to believe he was referring to Melissa Sandoval who was killed less than two weeks before and was last seen on the Boulevard getting into a light-colored Bronco or Blazer vehicle.

Quinland managed to escape and contacted authorities. Taylor was arrested for attempted murder and convicted in June of 1989 for nine years to life in prison. Taylor was released on parole in January of 2011.

Wayne Robert Amundson was extradited from the State of Wisconsin. He was on probation in Wisconsin for a sexual assault in 1989. DNA evidence, a yellow piece of rope matched the type Amundson used to pull cable through conduit, a right-handed glove found at White's murder scene which matched the type of gloves used by Amundson at the Cable Company where he worked, along with victims' statements connected Amundson in the attempted murder of Dolores Fernandez on December 29, 1986 and the murder of Melissa Gene White whose body was found two days later. Melissa was found close to the Pala Indian Reservation where Amundson previously lived with a family. He was tried and convicted and received a 16-years to life sentence in June of 1993. He came up for parole twice and was denied. He will be eligible once again in December of 2023.

Bryan Maurice Jones: On October 16, 1985 Jones raped, threatened to kill, and attempted to sodomize Bertha R. In 1987 Jones was convicted and sentenced to 22 years for the multiple acts. Prior to the 1987 conviction Jones committed the following acts:

On August 15, 1985, Jones struck up a conversation with Maria R. on El Cajon Boulevard. He offered to pay $20.00 for sex and took the bus with Jones to his apartment. After the sex Jones burst into the bathroom where Maria was showering, put a rope around her neck and began choking her. Maria lost consciousness and when she came to, he attacked her again. He told her she had to orally copulate him if she wanted to be released. Fearing for her life she complied and was released after he took his money back. Maria notified police and identified him at the scene. Jones was arrested and released a few days later.

Less than two weeks later on August 29, 1985, the body of Tara Simpson was found in a burning dumpster behind a business at 5100 El Cajon Boulevard. Her remains were burnt almost beyond recognition. An accelerant was used to ignite the contents of the dumpster. Evidence during the autopsy showed a traumatic injury to her nose and a knife-like wound to her abdomen. There was also evidence of petechial hemorrhages to the surface of her heart suggesting asphyxiation. Jones was tried for Simpson's murder, but it resulted in a hung jury leaning towards guilty.

On February 11, 1986, firefighters responded to another dumpster fire in the same alley a block from where Tara Simpson was found. In this dumpster the body of prostitute Trina Carpenter was found. She showed evidence of bruising on her body and around her neck. An accelerant was used in this case as well. She was placed in a duffle bag before she was set on fire. Two cotton balls were found with Carpenter's body one in her hand the other loose in the bag. They contained evidence of sperm and skin cells. Vaginal swabs produced the presence of spermatozoa as well as a high degree of acid phosphatase indicating seminal fluid. The night she was killed a neighbor heard a loud noise coming from the alley and looked out to see an older model blue car with oxidized paint near the dumpster. When the fire department responded, the vehicle fled the scene. Jones was charged with her murder, but it resulted in a hung jury leaning 11-1 for guilt.

Jo Ann Sweets was murdered and found in a dumpster on May 9, 1986 behind Jones' apartment close to where Trina Carpenter was found and where Maria R was assaulted. She was wearing a brassiere and blouse but was nude from the waist down. She suffered injuries to her face and neck. Her collar bone and neck were fractured. She died from strangulation. Carpet fibers found on JoAnn's blouse and on the mattress-pad were a match for the carpeting in Jones' apartment. Semen stains and skin cells on the bed sheet were a match for Jones. A palm print belonging to Jones was lifted off the trash bag and a latent print was lifted from the dumpster. Vaginal and oral swaps tested negative for sperm, but a rectal swap showed some sperm but it wasn't enough for testing. Jones was charged with first degree murder of Jo Ann Sweets with a special circumstance allegation he killed her in the commission or attempted commission of sodomy. Jones was convicted.

Sophia Glover was found August 15, 1986 rolled in a blanket, left on the parkway in the 2200 block of Madison Avenue, a block from Jones' mother's workplace on Mississippi Street. She sustained extreme injuries to head, neck and chest and died from asphyxia caused by strangulation. A vaginal swab produced a scant amount of spermatozoa. Rectal swabs showed spermatozoa and acid phosphatase, consistent with Jones'. He was convicted of her murder with an additional special circumstances allegation that it was accomplished during the commission or attempted commission of sodomy.

Evidence of Jones' prior conviction on Bertha R. was introduced where Bertha was picked up by Jones in a Blue Datsun 280Z, driven to the Wilsie apartment on Mississippi Street. After the initial attack she was driven to Fiesta Island in the same vehicle. Jones' sister owned a two-tone Blue Datsun 280Z car which Jones borrowed on occasion.

On October 20, 1986, four days after assaulting Bertha R., prostitute Karen M. was picked up by Jones driving a Blue/Grey Datsun 280Z car in the 2900 block of Imperial Avenue. He drove to the Wilsie house on Mississippi Street. Jones had a key to and would spend time there even when his mother Ann wasn't working. Karen M. was assaulted and reported it to the police, but they didn't believe her story and transported her to detox. A follow up by detectives led to charging Jones with attempted murder, forcible rape, sodomy and oral copulation in addition to a special circumstance allegation of multiple murders (Jo Ann Sweets and Sophia Glover.) Jones was arrested in 1992 while serving time at Corcoran State Prison convicted and sentenced to death on April 6, 1994. Jones now awaits execution at San Quentin Prison.

Kerry Lyn Dalton, Sheryl Ann Baker and Mark Lee Tompkins, killed Irene Melanie Louise May on June 26, 1988 in Live Oak Springs, an unincorporated community in East San Diego County. May moved in with Dalton after her husband was arrested and Child Protective Services found her an unfit mother, taking her three children away from her. When Dalton was away after being arrested for drugs, May sold Dalton's items to buy drugs. In a fit of rage, Dalton decided to do away with May. All three ganged up on her after Dalton accused her of stealing. May was tortured with electric shocks, stabbed with a knife, screwdriver and injected with battery acid. The body was removed and never found. All three suspects including the victim were heavy Methamphetamine users.

The murder weighed heavily on Baker who rolled over on Dalton and her boyfriend Tompkins in 1992. Baker indicated to authorities, Dalton took the body, dismembered it in parts and buried it on numerous Indian Reservations to make it difficult to locate. This case was controversial because murder was charged without physical evidence or a body produced. The only evidence was Baker's confession and a jailhouse snitch. Baker pled guilty to second degree murder and has since been released. Thompkins was found guilty of first-degree murder and is currently housed at Valley State Prison in Chowchilla, California. He was denied parole on May 25, 2011 and comes up for parole again in May of 2021.

Dalton was tried and convicted of first-degree murder with two special circumstances of lying in wait and torture. She was condemned to die by lethal injection in 1994. She is now on death row at the Central California Women's Facility in Chowchilla, California.

And finally, Ronald Elliot Porter was arrested for the choking and sexual assault of Annette Russell, a prostitute picked up hitchhiking by Porter in October of 1988, who told her he could take her as far as El Centro. Once inside Porter drove her to the Buckman Springs exit area where she was choked into unconsciousness and sexually assaulted. When she came to her pants were pulled down to her ankles and her blouse was pulled up, exposing her breasts. She was picked up by a passing Sheriff's unit who saw what appeared to be a Grey Honda leaving the area. He put out an all units broadcast of the vehicle. Porter's car was pulled over and he was arrested. A semen stain was found on Russell's blouse. He was charged with six felonies including attempted murder but pled out several days before going to trial. Porter pled to counts of assault and sexual battery. He was sentenced to four years in prison on April 4, 1989.

When a search warrant was served on Porter after the Russell arrest, a set of walkie talkies belonging to Kecia Betts were found in a storage shed. Porter kept linking up to the attack on her. Betts was picked up, choked and left for dead. A hair found in Bett's shoe matched hairs from Porter and well as the property from Betts found in Porters storage unit.

In addition, investigators were looking for the van Porter used in the Betts' attack. Porter's sister Carol Porter (Jones) used it occasionally. She was also in the North County of San Diego.

Porter was released 20 months later and was kept under 24 hours surveillance. After driving on the wrong side of the road and almost colliding with Task Force officers, he was arrested for violating his parole and returned to prison. In September of 1991 while back in prison, Porter was charged with the July 21, 1988 murder of Sandra Cwik, the June 30, 1986 murder of Carol Gushrowski, the November 1986 attempted murder of Kecia Betts (Gardner), the February 1988 attempted murder of Donna Abbott and Robin Brown, the March of 1988 attempted murder of Betty Bass and the May 1988 attempted murder of Maria Weidmark.

In the attacks on Donna Abbott and Robin Brown, footprints matching Porter's shoes and tire tracks matching a spare tire were evidenced. During the ride, the girls conversed with Porter who told Brown, he got out of the Marines in 1968. Records show Porter was released from the Marines in 1968. Abbott picked Porter from a "six pack" photo lineup but Brown couldn't do so.

Betty Bass was the next victim of Porters in March of 1988. She accepted a ride from him and was driven out past the town of Alpine in East San Diego County. He choked her, assaulted her and she was left for dead. Marlboro cigarette butts were found where Bass was assaulted along with fiber evidence matching Porter's vehicle.

Maria Weidmark was a housewife hitchhiking along Interstate 8 who accepted a ride from Porter. He told her he could take her as far as El Centro, a signature catchphrase he used with his victims. After stopping he choked Weidmark unconscious. She was able to identify Porter.

The judge dropped the Homicide of Carol Gushrowski due to insufficient evidence. It was a weak circumstantial case. Her body was found in the same Buckman Springs area where other bodies were dumped.

Porter was acquitted on the five attempted murders as the jury felt even though the victims were choked, assaulted and left for dead, it didn't meet the standard for attempted murder.

Come on folks! If your mother, wife, sister or daughter was choked, assaulted and left for dead on the roadway, or if it happened to you. what crime would you expect authorities to charge? Because the three-year statute of limitations had expired for charging simple assault, Porter was able to overcome the five attempted murder charges. Additionally, Porter was absent from work on the day Cwik was attacked and raped with a foreign object, causing her death from extreme hemorrhaging. Porter could provide no reason for his absence from work.

Porter was tried for the murder of Sandra Cwik and was convicted of second-degree murder on Cwik. He was convicted of rape with a foreign object on Bass. He was sentenced October 26, 1992 to 28 years to life. A sentence of 15 years to life for the killing of Cwik, eight years for rape with a foreign object on Betty Bass and, an additional five years for a prior felony conviction.

Although Porter was responsible for 13 other homicides including the murder of Donna Marie Gentile based on blood, hair, fibers, tire and footprints, it was decided not to try him for the others.

The case against Gentile was strong but the others were weak. It was felt if they lost cases against Porter, they wouldn't be able to prosecute him again due to the double jeopardy standard. The evidence against Porter and the other murders however was sufficient enough to consider the cases closed.

Dick Lewis wrote his own press releases and spoke at his own news conferences. I was told prior to his statement to the media, "Based on the evidence against Ronald Elliott Porter for the Gentile killing, it would certainly preclude us from charging anyone else." With the sentence Porter received it was felt he would never see the outside of a prison cell for the rest of his natural life. The people of the world would finally be safe from his savagery. Porter was denied Parole on three occasions. He will be eligible for parole again in December of 2022 where he will be 75 years of age.

At any age, Porter is a danger to anyone if released.

CHAPTER TWENTY-TWO

FORMER DISTRICT ATTORNEY ED MILLER LEARNS ABOUT ME

I WORKED in an office building which housed more than 20 attorneys, most of whom took advantage of my services. My role was like that of a Doctor making his rounds in a hospital. I'd drop in on them almost weekly and would walk out with either photo assignments, surveillances, court research, service of process or full-blown criminal or civil cases requiring complete workups. Life was good.

There were three attorneys just in my office, plus a building full of more attorneys across the street on one side and, another building across the street on the other side. My office was a half block away from the El Cajon Courthouse. I had more work coming to me than I ever imagined. I could pick and choose my assignments as they came in. I always refused to do Domestic Surveillance in Divorce cases unless children and drugs were involved or, a suspected case of child abuse or neglect was involved.

Most Judges weren't interested in the mud-slinging brought up in court in divorce. Their attitude was, if you can't make a marriage work, get out of it. I also usually turned down people who would state, "I want a picture of him cheating, so I can shove it in his face!"

I'd respond to them by saying, "All that's going to do is get your face slapped and, it'll cost you $500.00 to $1000.00 dollars. I can slap you for nothing and save you a lot of money. Spend it on a good attorney and get out of your situation. Courts really don't want to hear about your dirty laundry."

It was October of 1999; things were quieting down in San Diego. The Homicide Task Force had disbanded six years previously.

I was aware of Dick being diagnosed with leukemia. It was a horrible blow. I was in communication with Dick throughout his treatments and when he was at the City of Hope Hospital in Duarte, California. They were working on testing the latest treatments, but the survival rate was poor and eventually both of us realized the inevitable. Dick never gave up hope though, he was a fighter to the end.

One day while checking my mail I found a flyer regarding a fund-raising dinner. It involved the San Diego Law Enforcement Foundation. So, I thought I'd attend and maybe see some of my old cop friends. It was an optional costume dinner on Friday evening October 15, 1999. It was held at the Abbey special event facility on Fifth Avenue in downtown San Diego. Dinner was at 6:00 pm with an auction following and a prize for the best costume.

So, not knowing who might attend, I thought it better to go in disguise. I put on a black "Skyhawk" comic book character T-shirt with a white glow in the dark character.* I strapped my diving knife and sheath to my upper left arm and wore white artic camouflage pants that were bloused over my boots. On my face, I wore brown camouflage makeup. I went as a "Space Commando."

I arrived early and was met at the door by people I recognized from the Police Department. They weren't exactly people I would've associated with, and it might've created a stir or more if I was recognized. But I wasn't recognized. So, in the spirit of good will I looked them straight in the eye and shook their hands said hello as I walked into the room. I wasn't asked my name. I always made sure to shake hands with the opposition.

I bought a drink at the bar, picked my table and sat down. A few minutes later I heard some commotion at the area near the front door. I turned around and looked in that direction and saw a person I immediately recognized. He was with a lady and holding her arm as they walked in. Little did I know, this man and woman would come and sit at the table with me. He politely pulled a chair out for the woman.

Of all the people in San Diego, I ended up sitting at the same table with the Former District Attorney of San Diego County, Edwin J. Miller, Jr. and his wife Barbara. This was Dick's boss.

Mr. Miller stood and introduced himself and his wife, Barbara. I'd never met either one of them in public, but I recognized him from television and the Courthouse.

This was a real treat. I thought about what I might say to him and my mind was filled with questions. Miller had a firm handshake and shook my hand. I told him my name. I had no idea who would attend this event.

We ate dinner and I kept thinking to myself, say something you fool. Tell him what you did with Dick for seven years. This may be your only chance.

I leaned over the round table which seated eight people and said to Miller, "I'd like to discuss something regarding one of your Deputy District Attorneys and the Metropolitan Homicide Task Force.

Miller turned and looked at me saying, "You must be talking about Dick Lewis."

I was shocked, as if he was reading my mind. I didn't mention anyone in particular and there were three people who headed his San Diego Metropolitan Homicide Task Force at various times. Chuck Rogers started as the head of the Task Force followed by Bonnie Dumanis and finally Dick Lewis. But he seemed to know exactly who I was talking about.

I told Miller, Dick had discussed my case with a friend and former Homicide Sergeant from the San Bernardino Sheriff's Department when the two dined together in 1986.

I told him, Dick followed my case with the Police Department and asked his friend Don Hardy if I'd be willing to speak with him. Dick told me when we met I was set up by my department and he could prove it. The next seven years was history. I was afraid for an instant he would be upset at what Dick did for me, taking me under his wing all those years and making me privy to confidential information regarding the Task Force Investigations.

Mr. Miller looked at me and smiled. He said, "If you were under his wing for seven years you must've learned a ton from him." Dick taught him a thing or two during his 24 years as District Attorney. Miller spoke highly of Dick and told me so. He told me to my face, "Dick was my first choice to *ead the Task Force, but at the time I couldn't spare him."

Miller commended me for my efforts to clear my name, and to come forward with a suspect responsible for the Gentile homicide. He told me they wanted to charge Porter with all 14 homicides. Gentile's case was strong, but some of the other cases were not, and to try Porter for all the cases, was taking the chance of losing one on a technicality. That would preclude them under the double jeopardy standard from ever retrying him.

The subject turned to Dick's illness. Miller said, "It's a damn shame to hear about Dick having Leukemia, but Dick's a fighter and he'll come out on top."

Finally, he asked me what I planned on doing with all the information I amassed.

I told him someday I might write a book about everything.

Mr. Miller patted me on the back and said, "You write it, I'll buy it."

I was beaming with a grin from ear to ear and felt a warm sensation inside.

Unfortunately, Ed Miller died Sunday March 3, 2013 at the age of 87, from Liver Cancer. He was District Attorney for the County of San Diego for 24 years and left his mark.

DICK SUCCUMBS

On October 13, 2000, I lost a true friend to Leukemia. Dick Lewis, who was like a father to me, finally lost his year-long battle with Leukemia. Like my father, they both shared the same birthday of September 5' but they were eight years apart in age. Still, he was old enough to be my father.

Dick was tough, knowledgeable and a fighter. He knew where all the skeletons were hidden. He taught me how to better investigate a case. We spent countless hours together going over material regarding the Gentile Homicide and other murders which occurred at this time.

In my Chapter 14: My Lifesavers, I looked up to him as if he was a God. He didn't like what the department did to me one bit. So, he made it a priority to vindicate me. There was nothing Dick wouldn't do for me. After Dick would come to the Task Force secret headquarters* in Mission Valley, we'd meet for breakfast in La Mesa at the Bake House Restaurant. I'd be briefed on the current status of cases they were working. I learned a great many things about my department and people the District Attorney's office was well aware of at the time.

I was invited to Dick's house in Ramona numerous times and met his wife, Dottie.* In March of 2000 Dick came home from the hospital. We managed to have one more discussion when I saw him at home for the last time. Funny, I got the same reaction from Dick as I got from Miller. It was as if they knew what the other was thinking and what the other would say.

He'd lost a lot of weight and was frail and weak. I'm glad I could spend a valuable, cherished hour with him. The next day he returned to the City of Hope Hospital. I only spoke to him on the phone from this point forward. Dick was receiving the latest treatments for his type of Leukemia.

I recall a conversation I had with him about what to get my father for his upcoming 80th birthday. I wanted to do something special. He already had golf putters, ties, shirts and other clothing, but I told Dick this must be something different.

He asked me, "What do you think he would enjoy?"

I thought for a minute and said, "You know, he was in the Army Chemical Corps during the War in the Pacific and he was told he was subject to recall at any time. He never received his separation papers from the Army." I told Dick, "I'd like to get him officially released from the Army if it's even possible. I think there are much younger men they could use."

Dick turned to me and said, "You know, my brother Jerry, is a U.S. Congressman and he happens to head the Armed Services Committee, I'll ask if he can do anything."

A few days later, I received a conference call from Dick and his kid brother, Jerry.

Jerry told me, "The normal procedure is for the person in question to make the request himself, but I'll see what I can do."

I gave Jerry my dad's information and his address in Palm Springs.

On Tuesday September 5th, I called my dad to wish him a happy birthday. I asked, "Dad, are you going to do anything special for your birthday?"

Dad replied, "Yes as a matter of fact, I need to buy a couple picture frames."

I said, "For what?"

Not only did Dick's brother come through for me and get him officially discharged from the United States Army, but he also received a birthday card from the President of the United States, something normally only done when someone attains the age of 100.

Dad was absolutely floored.

So many doors were opened for me thanks to Dick. A wrongful death case of a girl who died when doctors overdosed her with cocaine for a Rhinoplasty* was finally investigated by the California Medical Board of Quality Assurance. Cases previously rejected by the District Attorneys' office were reopened and prosecuted.

There wasn't a door he couldn't open for me. He used to call me "Tiger." Jeff Dusek, his lead prosecutor for the Task Force said he called everyone "Tiger" when talking to them.

To this day it still stings when I remember the day of his passing on October 13, 2000.*

What he did for me, clearing my name which lead to my vindication with law enforcement, the vast knowledge I gleaned from him, educating me on how to be a better investigator and giving me an inside track on one of the most successful serial killer Task Forces in the Country. It's a debt of friendship I'll never be able to repay.

Rest in Peace my friend and thank you for everything.

CHAPTER TWENTY-THREE

OH, WHAT A TANGLED WEB WE WEAVE

THE NAME of this chapter is often thought to be from Shakespeare, but it's actually from Marmion, a poem written by Sir Walter Scott. Think about it. A tangled web like a spider, with lines running vertically and horizontally. All leads back to a central core, where the spider sits, waiting for his prey to be snared. Now, think of every silken line as a strategically placed "good old boy" located on the outer reaches, like drones loyal to a queen bee. Each one lets the spider in the center know when prey might threaten their little kingdom.

The San Diego Police Department had many of these "webs."

Much of this book was written based on my personal experience, the records I've kept, my personal documentation and the events seared in my memory. They've remained in safekeeping in seven, dusty, cardboard boxes in a storage unit for all these years. I knew about some of the "webs," but going through everything after all these years to write this book, I had no idea how complex the "web" of the San Diego Police Department was, with the sole purpose of protecting the guilty parties.

I realized I was playing against a stacked deck, but I never completely understood the total magnitude of it until 2018. Yes, 33 years later when I finally dedicated myself to writing this book and re-discovered it in a way that surprised me, the webs of social media which didn't exist way back in the 1980s. One example is Facebook.

My online, social media research only resulted in touching the tip of the iceberg. I decided to check for individuals involved in the Gentile investigation back in the day. These friendships on the force weren't recently formed; they'd been in place for many years.

The drones and queen bees in this web were long-time alumni of the "good old boy system" dating back to the 1970's and 1980's.

I made up a pseudonym and started a Facebook account just to do a little online investigating. I began checking for accounts under the names of people associated with the Gentile investigation.

Take Carl Black, he was my Lieutenant back in 1983 and 1984. But what was his history? He doesn't have a Facebook account. Nor does Black show up under any other social media platforms unless it's under another name. But, I discover he and his old buddy Kenny Hargrove go way back. They worked on the same squad together before moving up in the Department. They both had numerous dalliances with women. Both were disciplined for their association and unprofessional activities involving a nurse, from the now defunct Physicians and Surgeons Hospital once located in San Diego.

Their squad was broken up and several officers were "quietly fired." The matter was kept under wraps and never discussed. Some squad members have since passed, but some are still around and have broken their silence.

The department was well aware of their past liaisons but instead they chose to "quietly" handle it rather than follow their own policies.

In 1981, Carl Black was a Lieutenant in Communications.* He was the subject of a sexual harassment investigation involving a dispatcher while working there. I personally discussed the matter with the dispatcher who was deathly afraid of him. She was visibly uncomfortable when reliving the incident with me in an effort to get a better profile about his work and his fooling around at work.

He had personnel working beneath him. Three Sergeants who also worked in communications at this time included Sergeant Glenn Breitenstein, Connie Van Putten and Jerry Sanders. Breitenstein* later was involved in investigating me when he moved to Internal Affairs. Van Putten moved up to the rank of Lieutenant and became one of my Lieutenants at Eastern during my investigation. Finally, Jerry Sanders moved up and become the department's Police Chief years later.

They were acutely aware their co-worker was under investigation and Breitenstein was happy to do pretty much anything to save Black's hide, because they were "buddies." But he was anything but impartial when conducting my investigation.

Black, apparently shot his mouth off once too often telling the wrong person he thought he could trust Breitenstein would brazenly approach him with a "trump card" to use just in case he needed to bail himself out and save his job.

Black conveyed to this friend in a phone conversation when Breitenstein worked the field, he caught a well-liked Officer who later became a Chief Officer in the act of having sex with a minor while on duty.

Black first received a ten-day suspension for his involvement with Gentile, regarding the Colorado river trip. But he was finally terminated after he lied about giving her money, paying her medical bills, co-signing for her bail when she was arrested and, contacting a Probation Officer on Gentile's behalf.

Instead of going away quietly, he requested a Chief's Appeal with

Bill Kolender, the Chief of Police back then. Miraculously, his job and his neck were spared at the eleventh hour. What was said in the interview between those two men will never be known. Bill Kolender died a few years back from Alzheimer's and Black isn't talking. Did he use Breitenstein's "trump card" to save his job? It would've taken some pretty threatening or scandalous information for a lone Chief of Police to take the massive step of reversing the Department's decision after all the internal investigative work done on Black.

If you recall in Chapter 11, I introduced Lieutenant Richard Boas who stated he overheard some high-ranking officials making the corrupt statement outside his office, "If we don't fire Black, then Avrech's got a case."

Apparently, this was a highly complex decision for the Department. Based on what I discovered many years later, it involved numerous "football huddles" and collective brainstorming. The parties involved looked at all the possible scenarios and complications they faced if Black or I were terminated. Who could hurt them the worst outside the Department? Ultimately it was decided Black had several "God-fathers" within the department and I had none. Once again, corruption won out over integrity.

Now, during Black's investigation which I wasn't privy to, he was transferred out to Northern Division and was interviewed by Captain Keith Enerson. Their relationship was an unknown to all the people I spoke with, however Enerson and Black's buddy, Kenny Hargrove (Gentile's date at the Colorado River) are still friends today on Facebook. Again, I don't think they became friends recently. They had a long-lasting friendship that went back years ago together at the department.

Now Hargrove accompanied Gentile, Black and another Sergeant, Jeff Fellows to the Colorado River for a boisterous weekend of fun and frolicking.

Why would Black make the move to procure a prostitute for a buddy? This question unearths many more questions. If for no other reason, wouldn't Black be at all concerned about the possibility of his friend catching a sexually transmitted disease from a young woman who was an active prostitute? You certainly would think so. Friends don't subject friends to nasty inconveniences like STD's.

Why would Ken Hargrove later play dumb claiming he didn't know Gentile was a prostitute? Because, playing innocent was his only defense as to why he had sex with her and the Department actually bought his lame excuse.

A combined decision must've been made somewhere along the way to overlook Hargrove's indiscretion again, because when I tried to expose this episode, it made me a bigger fish to fry and an even bigger threat to the department.

Looking at Hargrove and his connections today, he is still friends with Fellows on Facebook.

When on Facebook, one would think some decision-making is done when a person makes a request to "friend" you. People agree to everyone who wants to "friend" them, right? No, I don't think so. This is especially true for women. If possible, you at least check out their profile.

- Are they male or female?
- Are they married or single?
- What is their motivation for the request before you decide and click "accept?"
- Do they have hobbies or interests in the same arena of interest to you?

There is some cognitive thought involved before making this decision. Facebook and other social media memberships aren't just a numbers game where people arbitrarily pick anyone who contacts them on a whim.

So why are so many of the people involved in my investigation still friendly with one another? Because, they're all cut from the cloth known as the "good old boys" club. They back one another up whether they're right or wrong. I could mention others and their relationships on social media, but there's no need to beat a dead horse with the point. I think I've proven my case.

CHAPTER TWENTY-FOUR

MEETING DONNA GENTILE'S COUSIN ANITA

When Donna Gentile's family received notification of her death, they were outraged. They wanted answers and they wanted them fast. Her brother, Louis wanted a congressional investigation into criminal wrongdoing by the San Diego Police Department. It was their opinion based on newspaper accounts police officers were involved in her demise.

It made sense to them. She went to Internal Affairs with trumped up allegations against me to save my Lieutenant, her "Sugar Daddy" in the hope of getting her sentence for Prostitution reduced. Then after testifying for the city at my Civil Service hearing, her lifeless body was found in East San Diego County.

In February of 2017, I set up a blog to introduce people to the book I was planning to write, to discuss the truth about the killing of Donna Marie Gentile. The people of San Diego were made to think because she was a police informant at one time, she was killed by the cops. This was planted in the minds of San Diegans in breathless daily coverage across all media outlets. Between what she was told, the people of San Diego, what the Police Department put out in press releases and what they kept close to the vest or refused to comment upon left little doubt.

On June 26, 2017, I received a message on my blog, (acop-scop@blogspot.com) from Anita De Francesco, Donna's first cousin. Anita informed me, she was writing a book about Donna's life and the letters Donna wrote her, before her murder.

At first, I didn't know what to think. Was this someone's idea of a joke or was it for real? I made several attempts to contact Donna's brother Louis but was unsuccessful. I went to the website Anita left me on the blog which contained a phone number. I called and spoke with her. Now, I at least had a family member willing to talk with me. I was curious as to what she might have. I was a little hesitant to call her because I got the impression, she might think I had something to do with Donna's death. We continued to email, text and had several phone conversations. Over time we developed an understanding and respect for one another and became good friends.

During this period, Anita told me about an annual memorial service dedicated to sex workers who were slain the previous year across the United States. December 17 is the day this is observed in all 50 states. The significance of the date is the week in 2003, Gary Ridgway, the infamous Green River Killer from Seattle, Washington was sentenced for the killing of over 49 women. The program scheduled included various speakers talking about the need to curb violence against sex workers and attempt to establish a working relationship to bridge the gap between police and prostitutes.

While I'm in favor of programs for stopping violence against sex workers, I'm not a proponent of legalizing prostitution. The courts should have greater sentencing guidelines for anyone who harms a prostitute. Unfortunately, many promises have been made by the bureaucrats, but few have been kept.

In anticipation of speaking, I prepared to talk about "bridging the gap" between the police and prostitutes so they can feel safe reporting crimes to the police without fear of retaliation or harassment. Back in April of 1984, when I was in the field, we agreed to an understanding with the girls. "We are both out here trying to make a living, but if our paths crossed, we have to enforce the law. At the same time we are here to protect the citizens of San Diego and if you need assistance, we're here to help you."

On the suggestion of my squad partner, Lou David Rawles, we passed out notebooks and little golf pencils to the girls on El Cajon Boulevard. They understood if two or more girls were on a street corner and a "John" picked one up, the other girl would write down the license plate number and a description of the person. In this way if she ever turned up assaulted, missing or killed, we'd have some information to work with in solving the case. It was such a simple thing to do, but it was a hard sell for the girls. Their attitude was, "It won't happen to me."

No sooner did we implement this and we put this to use. On April 11, 1984 two prostitutes, Sheila Jackson and Debra Coleman summoned a passing police vehicle. They reported a male driver in a 1980's silver station wagon with orange license plates who picked them up. He showed them a five-pointed "star" badge and asked them to feel a gun belt under the passenger seat of his vehicle. He exposed himself and threatened to arrest them if they didn't provide him with sexual favors.

My Sergeant, Harold Goudarzi was stopped and put out an all units broadcast for the vehicle. My reserve partner Steve Tompkins was working with me that night and driving in the area when we saw a vehicle pass in the opposite direction matching the description. The driver stared at us intently as he passed.

I told my partner to make a "U" turn and pursue the vehicle. I radioed for cover units. While following the suspected vehicle, he ran a red light and drove at a high rate of speed. We caught up to him behind other traffic at the next light and performed a "Hot Stop" of the vehicle. I got out with my shotgun and held him at bay until other units arrived. He was removed from the vehicle and cuffed.

Steve asked the suspect, "Where's the gun?"

The suspect, Daniel Orin Reed, responded saying, "I got a 4-inch 38, revolver under the passenger seat."

Recovered were 12 rounds of 38 caliber hollow point ammunition, a Miranda Admonishment card, an Escambia County, Florida Sheriff's five-pointed star badge and a Sheriff's ID card. The gun was run and found to be stolen from Pittsburgh, Pennsylvania.

Even back then simple cooperation with the girls using primitive methods were successful in taking a possible future serial killer and another gun off the streets. Today, girls in many states have a "bad date sheet" to alert other girls and police of these individuals.

I wasn't able to speak, however I read the names of the slain women across the nation in 2017. They were as follows:

Diana Hemmingway (46) South Florida December 20, 2016

Patricia Phelps aka Peppermint Patty (48) Anchorage, Alaska August 16, 2017

Jessica Newcomb (20) Mobile, Alabama June 16, 2017

Isabell Pam (43) Huntsville, Alabama February 26, 2017

Jennifer Ann Wilson (50) Tucson, Arizona September 18, 2017

Gemmel Moore (26) West Hollywood, California July 27, 2017

Jarrae Esteep (21) found dead March 14, 2017

Josephine Vargas (34) last seen October 24, 2017

Kianna Jackson (20) last seen October 21, 2017

Martha Anaya (28) last seen November 28, 2017

Sable Pickett (19) Anaheim, California April 14, 2017

Brittney Taylor (19) Tamarac, Florida May 25, 2017

Essence Owens (23) Groveland, Florida August 22, 2017

Amber Elizabeth Carruthers (32) Orlando, Florida June 17, 2017

Hannah Darlene Midyette (21) Jacksonville, Florida March 30, 2017

Olympia Cerruti (34) Daytona, Florida September 23, 2017

Bridget Shie (19) Atlanta, Georgia February 1, 2017

Ashley Brandeberry (29) Waikiki Beach, Hawaii April 24, 2017

Desiree Robinson (15) Chicago, Illinois December 24, 2016

Kayla Denham (25) Livingston, Louisiana June 9, 2017

Alphonza Watson (38) Baltimore, Maryland March 22, 2017

April Ellis (34) Baltimore, Maryland March 23, 2017

Renia Rodriguez (19) Braintree, Massachusetts June 22, 2017

Tobi Lynn Stanfill Albuquerque, New Mexico May 19, 2017

Unidentified Woman Bronx, New York January 17, 2017

Yang Song (38) Flushing, New York

Joanne Brown (33) Montclair, New Jersey Last seen October 22, 2016 S.I.C.

Sara Butler (20) Montclair, New Jersey Last seen November 23, 2016 S.I.C.

Robin Edwards (19) Philadelphia, Pennsylvania December 21, 2016 S.I.C.

Ashley Ugoletti (27) Westmoreland County, Pennsylvania

Rhonda Wells (44) Memphis, Tennessee January 13, 2017

Jessica Lewis (28) Memphis, Tennessee January 13, 2017

Stephanie L. Garcia (34) San Antonio, Texas January 22, 2017

Brandi Seals (26) Houston, Texas December 13, 2017

T he following day I spent some time with Anita before leaving to head back home. I brought documents and information to bolster her book and fill in the gaps regarding the Gentile investigation. I needed to convince her I wasn't responsible for her death.

Anita is of the opinion I was just the department's collateral damage and got caught up in the middle of this scandal.

In the final analysis, we both agree Donna, no matter what she did, as well as other slain sex workers, didn't deserve to die such a violent death.

Since the writing of this chapter, I was asked to return this year and read off the names of the dead.

I flew to Philadelphia on December 13, 2018 and participated in the December 17 event. It was held in the evening at PhilaMOCA, the Philadelphia Mausoleum of Contemporary Art. While reading the names of the dead after last year's December 17 reading, the program coordinator Melanie Dante Goodman was on stage with red "coban" wrapped around her mouth to represent the victims who were silenced and unheard.* I was able to share the Daniel Orin Reed arrest with the group at this time.*

Unfortunately, Anita chose to launch her book in November of 2018 and all the information we discussed regarding never before seen documents I provided were released prior to the publishing of this book. Despite all the evidence Homicide Task Force officers had on Ronald Elliott Porter for the Gentile murder, I was physically there and briefed almost daily for seven years, it makes more sense to Anita to continue to see her cousin as a martyr and she died for a cause. The alternative narrative? Donna was a street prostitute who took too many chances, got into the wrong car and forfeited her most precious possession, her life.

CONCLUSION

My prayers were answered. By helping solve the Gentile murder I was vindicated in 1993 when The San Diego Metropolitan Homicide Task Force made the announcement after investigating the facts. "That no past or present San Diego Police Officer was involved in the murder of Donna Marie Gentile."

However, with the writing of this book it also finally vindicates me with the press, the San Diego Police Department and the People of San Diego. I only expected a higher authority beyond the police department, namely the San Diego County District Attorney's Office, the trier of fact and the sifter of truth to unravel the nightmare which befell me. I never in my wildest dreams expected to take such an active role in unravelling what happened to Donna Marie Gentile as I did.

I'd like to commend the Task Force for the overall job they did. To those reports which sprang from the citizens of San Diego accusing the Task Force of dragging their feet, not doing their job, money wasted, or cover-ups and the like, I say, "Not so. Not by a long shot."

You might fall back on the premise most of the murders were committed in the County and not the City of San Diego; then you might blame the Sheriff's Department and not the Police Department. But this wouldn't be a fair assumption, either.

Remember, most of the murders occurred in San Diego before the formation of the Task Force on September 1, 1988. I suggest to you in 1988 when the Task Force was formed and agencies started putting their heads together and left their egos at the door, things were accomplished. Most of the murders were solved three or more years after they occurred, where the solvability factor diminishes greatly. There were a few bad apples, but they were dealt with accordingly and managed to not spoil the whole barrel.

To the next of kin, who felt justice wasn't served or it was impartial, I apologize for your feelings. To others who finally received favorable news, I'm glad you were afforded some form of closure about the death of your loved one.

To others who weren't convinced no matter how hard they tried, I can't help you.

Suspects charged with other crimes while already in prison were found guilty and charged after long awaited evidence came back after testing or, when live victims connected them to additional crimes. If not for the live victims coming forward, many of the murderers might still be walking the streets today. Additional charges were leveled at suspects, not for the purpose of clearing cases. They were properly investigated and evidence was thoroughly collected, and laboratory tested.

AUTHOR'S MESSAGE TO ALL

For readers in law enforcement or seeking future employment, I leave you with this message regarding the accountability of a ranking officer versus the foot soldier. They should be cut from the same cloth. However, in my case there were two different rule books used.

A department will trust you to do the job for them, but the gate only swings in one direction. Be honest be right but don't expect to trust them. They may have other agendas.

Rather than show parity on disciplinary decisions. They will sway towards the public image rather than tell the truth.

It is not shameful to admit when you are in the wrong. It shows you're human and not perfect and strive to do better by exacting change. However, it is shameful to coverup and conceal the truth to show a false sense of propriety.

Larry S. Avrech

January 31, 2019

BIBLIOGRAPHY BY CHAPTER

Chapter 1:

Clance, Homer "Nude body said to be call girls. Woman figured in firing, demotion of police officers." *San Diego Union,* July 4, 1985 B-3.

No Byline, "Woman's body found." *San Diego Union,* June 25, 1985 B-3.

Chikatilo, Andrei, Wikipedia, https://en.wikipedia.org/wiki/Andrei, Chikatilo, March 12, 2018'

Chapter 10:

The San Diego Police Officers Association, Inc. *"The San Diego Police Department Commemorative Album,"* 1889-1981 Communications Section, pages 219-220.

Chapter 11:

No Byline, "Woman's body found." Ibid, *San Diego Union,* June 25, 1985 B-3.

Chapter 13:

The Book of Psalms, New King James Version, *"The Holy Bible"* Psalm 7 page 626, 1982.

The Book of Psalms, New King James Version. *"The Holy Bible"* Psalm 54 page 656, 1982.

Blair, Tom "Once A Cop." *San Diego Union,* November 7, 1985 B-1.

Chapter 14:

Stryker-Meyer, John "Once a murder suspect, former cop now a PI." *Oceanside Blade-Tribune,* January 1995, B-1.

Yelp, picture of the *"Marine Room Restaurant of La Jolla, California."* January 2018. https://m.yelp.com

Chapter 15:

Gunston, Bill *"The Great Book of Modern Warplanes."* New York, Portland House 1987.

Chapter 16:

Google Earth, Street View, *"Ronald Elliot Porter's Apartment Complex"* at 4346 52nd Street, San Diego, 1984/2018. https://www.google.com

Google Earth, Street View, *"7-Eleven® Store at 5202 El Cajon Boulevard."* Just up the street from Porter's Apartment, 1984/2018. https://www.google.com

Chapter 19:

Stamper, Norman *"Breaking Rank, A Top Cop's Expose of the Dark Side of American Policing."* New York, Nation Books, 2005 pages 234-235.

Taylor, Jeanne *"The Diary of Jeanne Taylor, San Diego Police Department."* March 28, 1980-September 10, 1981, pages 1-57.

Chapter 22:

Google Earth, Street View, *"Secret Homicide Task Force Headquarters."* Mission Valley 1988/2018. https://www.google.com

Chapter 23:

The San Diego Police Officers Association, Inc. Ibid, *"The San Diego Police Department Commemorative Album,*1889-1981, Communications Section, pages 219-220.

A

K

P

Worth's on The Boulevard, 78

Wright, J. Volah, 180-1

Written Reprimand, 29, 31

Wrongful Death Cases, 130

Y

Yacolt, Washington, 190

Yellow Cab

Company, 127

Scandal, 92

Yuma, 43

Medical Center, 43

Z

Zavala, Felix, 23

Zerbe, Pat, 143

Zimmerman (Sgt.), 37-8, 42, 105, 123

#

1973 Chevrolet Caprice, 29

1977 Datsun F-10, 29

312-John Avrech, 25

38 Caliber Hollow Point, 206, 248

4346 52nd Street #6, 162